2,002 Romantic Ideas

Special Moments You Can Share with the One You Love

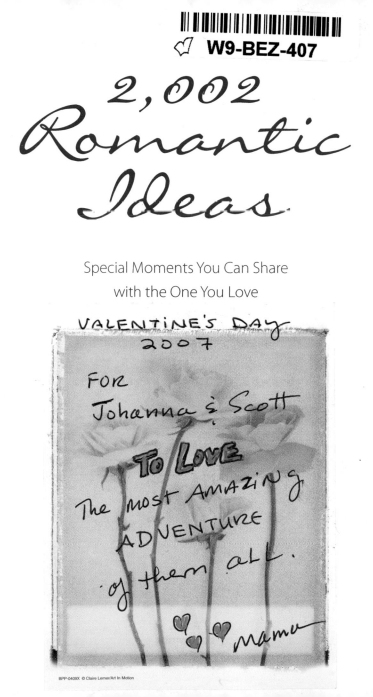

VALENTINE'S DAY
2007

FOR
Johanna & Scott

TO LOVE
The most AMAZING
ADVENTURE
of them all.

♥ ♥ ♥ mama

This book is dedicated to Andrew and we hope that your life will be filled with much love and romance.

∞

To love is to receive a glimpse of heaven.
~KAREN SUNDE

Library of Congress Cataloging-in-Publication Data
Haynes, Cyndi.
2,002 romantic ideas : special moments you can share with the one you love / by Cyndi Haynes and Dale Edwards.
p.   cm.
Includes bibliographical references
ISBN 1-59337-454-2 (alk. paper)
1. Man-woman relationships--Miscellanea. 2. Marriage--Miscellanea.
3. Love--Miscellanea. I. Title: Two thousand two romantic ideas. II. Title: Two thousand and two romantic ideas. III. Edwards, Dale, 1958- IV. Title.

HQ801.H373 2005
306.7--dc22

2005021908

This book is available at quantity discounts for bulk purchases.
For information, please call 1-800-289-0963..

Dear Reader:

*R*omance is back in style and burning brighter than ever.
Singles and married people alike are beginning to realize
just how important true romance is to the overall happiness
level of their entire lives. People want to have fun, feel special, and make
their partner feel loved, and that is what this book is all about. We have a
list of more than 2,000 ways to tweak your romantic life and get things
moving in the right direction. Whether you are in a brand new relationship or celebrating your twentieth wedding anniversary, we want
you to add some sparkle to your love life by trying some of the romantic
ideas from our book. Be creative—find ideas that speak to your sense of
romantic style and go for it! Love truly does make the world go around
and all you have to do is break out of your rut and have some fun. After
all, what do you have to lose? We know that you have everything to gain
by putting a little romance into your relationship.

Much romance,

Cyndi and Dale

*Wherever you go,
go with all your heart.*
—Confucius

1. Start with the basics:
   - ✦ Send flowers.
   - ✦ Give candy.
   - ✦ Surprise with gold jewelry.
   - ✦ Bring stuffed toys.
   - ✦ Play romantic CDs.
   - ✦ Date each other often.

2. Flirt only with your sweetheart. This is basic Romance 101.

3. Reenact the best date that the two of you have ever had. If it worked the first time, it should spice things up the second go around.

4. Remember to celebrate all your anniversaries:
   - ✦ First date
   - ✦ First kiss
   - ✦ Children's birthdays
   - ✦ Engagement
   - ✦ Wedding

5. Place a romantic stamp on the envelope whenever you send greeting cards to your mate.

Life has no joy nobler than that of love.
—**Author Unknown**

6. Make a toast to each other every time you drink champagne together. If you haven't had a celebration in a while, turn tonight into a special occasion by purchasing a nice bottle of champagne to share with your sweetie.

7. Give your love one of the best gifts you can give: your time. Don't confuse quality time with quantity of time. Make sure that you have plenty of both.

8. Send an old-fashioned telegram to your love expressing your feelings. Send another one inviting him or her out on a date.

9. Fall in love with each other all over again. Remember why you fell in love in the beginning.

10. Set out to overwhelm her by sending two dozen roses instead of the usual one dozen.

11. Learn what your mate thinks is romantic instead of always doing what you think is romantic. Ask questions. Look for clues. Listen closely to what he or she says. Ask his or her friends for help.

12. Get up early and watch the sunrise together.

13. Frame your favorite love note from your sweetheart. Display it proudly on your nightstand.

14. Get rid of all the tangible reminders of your old loves. Now the hard part: Forget all about your old loves. You don't need all of that old baggage.

15. When the two of you shop together, treat her to something she would love to have but is too practical to purchase. Splurge. Be extravagant.

16. Spend the longest night of the year (December 21) together. Plan a super-romantic date. Get out-of-the-box on your plans.

17. Compliment her in front of her mother, sisters, friends, and coworkers. She will love you for it! They will love you for it!

18. Dress up for an evening at home together. Remember that the person you want to impress the most is your significant other, so make the effort for each other.

19. Give her a subscription to the beautiful magazine *Romantic Homes*. Work together to make some romantic changes around your home.

20. When your love is too busy to go out, bring home dinner from his or her favorite restaurant.

21. Late at night, whisper your wildest fantasies to your partner. If you are the shy type, rehearse it before you say it.

22. Every time your mate does something special for you, write a nice thank-you note.

23. Plan little surprises for each other throughout the year. Don't limit your romantic gestures just to Valentine's Day.

24. Head over to the library for books, tapes, and magazines on ways to improve your love life. You will be inspired by all of the romantic tips you can easily find there.

25. Learn the fine art of pillow talk. Practice makes perfect.

26. Whenever you accept an award, be sure to acknowledge the contribution that your mate has made to your achievements. Make him or her feel appreciated and special.

27. To help you be more romantic and creative, work on developing the right side of your brain. Trust your intuition. Trust your hunches. Try a new approach to love.

28. Work harder on your love life than you do on your career. Your whole life will improve when your love life improves.

29. Seal all your love letters with a kiss (SWAK).

30. Create a romantic jigsaw puzzle using a love letter, poem, or song written on heavy paper or cardboard.

31. Give up the silly and unhealthy notion of "the perfect mate." It puts too much pressure on the relationship. After all, we are just human.

32. Host a rooftop picnic for two by moonlight.

33. Spend the weekend photographing each other all over town. Give the pictures as gifts, put them in your wallets or on your desks at work, and use them to create a great collage.

34. Set your alarm clock for fifteen minutes earlier than usual and spend the time just snuggling. It is a great way to start the day.

35. Choose a song that has a special meaning for your relationship and make it "your song."

36. Romance really is about the little things, so why not give him or her a Valentine Pez dispenser? It will bring back some happy childhood memories.

37. When you can't be together, send an instant message to your mate.

38. Write a love song for your sweetheart (you don't have to be good—it is the thought that counts).

ROMANTIC RULE #1
Make time for romance. Schedule it. Block out time on your calendar for it.

39. When you double-date, always go out with fun, upbeat couples. You want your friends to add to your enjoyment of the date, not to distract from it.

40. Have a "money is no object" date at least every few months. Go out and be wildly extravagant. Treat your love like royalty.

41. Carry your love's picture in your wallet and proudly show it to friends and family when your lover is with you.

42. During the Christmas season, send a bouquet of mistletoe and ask your sweetheart to use it for your lips only. Purchase another bouquet and hang it in your doorway.

43. Right now, put this book down and call your mate just to say hello.

44. Mark your mate's calendar with your birthday and all your "anniversaries."

45. Give a DVD library of wonderfully romantic movies.

46. For a little touch of affection, slip a greeting card under his or her pillow tonight.

47. Design a unique and personal greeting card on your computer and color printer. Mail it to your love interest tomorrow.

48. Give your partner one gift for each of the twelve days of Christmas. (Do not make them match the ones given in the song—he or she will think that you have lost your mind.)

49. Buy an outdoor fireplace and put it to good use for long romantic evenings in front of the fire. Talk, snuggle, and stay connected by the glow of your own backyard fire pit.

50. Drop by your significant other's office with a fun, quirky little gift.

51. Stop putting romance off to the weekends. Try to be romantic seven days a week. Your mate will love you for it!

52. For men: Know the five gifts that women request the most:
    - ✦ Jewelry
    - ✦ Perfume
    - ✦ Lingerie
    - ✦ Clothing
    - ✦ Handbags

53. For women: Know the five gifts that men request the most:
    - ✦ Clothing
    - ✦ Sports equipment
    - ✦ Gift certificates
    - ✦ Tickets
    - ✦ Stereo equipment

Love has the patience to endure
The fault it sees but cannot cure.
—Edgar A. Guest

54. Dare to be different and unique from all other lovers. Don't be a carbon copy of someone else. Be true to your inner Cupid.

55. In early February, go to your local card shop and stock up on romantic gift bags and gift wrap to use throughout the year.

56. Explore the whole wide world hand-in-hand.

57. Trim her bangs. Trim his mustache.

58. Promise him forever.

59. Give to her forever!

60. Present her with an artist's sketch of your honeymoon hotel. Include a letter telling some of your favorite memories from that special time in your lives.

61. Be a devoted, old-fashioned kind of lover. It can't be beat!

62. Keep in mind that research proves cuddling and snuggling are as important as sex.

63. In church on Sunday, share a hymnal with your sweetheart.

64. Treat yourselves to a special meal, such as Chateaubriand just for two.

65. Return to your honeymoon hotel and arrange to stay in the same room.

66. Reach out to your partner in:
    - ✦ Good times
    - ✦ Bad times
    - ✦ Romantic times

67. Give him or her a big ego by giving two compliments instead of just one. Just remember to always give compliments that will be appreciated by your significant other.

68. When you have to be couch potatoes and watch television, at least curl up together.

69. Spend all your leisure time together this weekend. Let each of you plan at least one activity.

70. When he or she has to be in the hospital, send a plant each day of the stay.

71. Cherish your love. Look up the true meaning of this word and work at loving your spouse in this wonderful manner.

72. Never use a romantic gift or gesture as a bribe. We shouldn't even have to tell you this!

73. Teach your parrot to say sweet nothings.

74. Frame your baby pictures together.

75. Always reserve the "best" table in the restaurant for your dinner dates. Call weeks in advance if you have to, but make the effort.

76. Send a little romantic memento after a special date. Try to send something that has special significance to the date.

77. Touch each other often throughout the day. This will give you both more feelings of closeness and togetherness.

78. Monogamy: the only way to live happily ever after. Print this on your heart and keep it there.

79. Always act glad to meet/greet your mate even after a hard day at work or with the kids. Don't meet your mate with problems spilling from your lips.

80. Mail great date ideas to his or her office. Try one new date a month.

All love that has not friendship for its base
is like a mansion built upon the sand.
—ELLA WHEELER WILCOX

81. Learn to love yourself so that you can truly be lovable to your mate.

82. Romantic mistakes that we don't want you to make:
    + Forgetting birthdays
    + Forgetting anniversaries
    + Being too uptight
    + Being practical in matters of the heart
    + Trying too hard to please
    + Picking an unworthy love interest
    + Going into debt for love's sake
    + Not being true to yourself

83. Purchase a quiet outdoor heater for late-night dinners under the stars. Take advantage of the beautiful harvest moons without the chill.

84. Keep courting each other for the rest of your lives! Never take each other for granted.

85. Hire a band and caterer for your next anniversary celebration even if it is just for the two of you at home.

86. Skip the prenuptial agreement. How unromantic can you get!

87. Buy a $200 bouquet of her favorite flowers. Knock her off her feet!

88. For a touch of Hollywood-style romance, rent:
    + *Ghost*
    + *The American President*
    + *Roman Holiday*
    + *Father of the Bride*
    + *Seems like Old Times*
    + *The Mirror Has Two Faces*
    + *Gone with the Wind*
    + *Something's Gotta Give*
    + *The Runaway Bride*
    + *Sweet Home Alabama*
    + *Sabrina*
    + *Sleepless in Seattle*
    + *Funny Girl*
    + *You've Got Mail*
    + *Titanic*
    + *The Wedding Planner*
    + *Somewhere in Time*
    + *The Truth About Cats and Dogs*

89. Talk at breakfast instead of just reading the newspaper in silence. Or snuggle up and share the paper.

90. Order romantic bumper stickers that express your feelings but won't embarrass your mate.

91. Place a love note inside a helium-filled balloon. Take it to her office and let her be the envy of all of her coworkers.

92. Make her feel like a princess by presenting her with a tiara. Costume or bridal shops will be able to help you with this one.

93. Never call your unromantic mate unromantic. Just say that he or she is romantically challenged.

94. For Halloween, dress up like a famous couple. Yes, even Raggedy Ann and Andy will do, and they are easy costumes to make.

95. Don't let rainy days put a damper on your passion. Dance, kiss, and walk in the rain. Or at least share an umbrella.

Love is a gross exaggeration of the differences between one person and everybody else.
—GEORGE BERNARD SHAW

96. Share a piece of wedding cake at the next wedding you attend. Make it even more romantic by feeding it to each other.

97. Put a little romance into the evening meal by cooking with heart-shaped pasta.

98. Go on another honeymoon. Repeat often! You can never have too many honeymoons as long as they are with the same spouse!

99. Make a lunch date for his favorite restaurant for today or tomorrow at the latest.

100. Look for great romantic specials the week before Valentine's Day at hotels and restaurants. Take advantage of some of them.

101. Give him books about his hobbies and interests to show that you support his other "loves."

102. Disconnect the doorbell at your busy home for a night of uninterrupted romance.

103. Kiss her awake in the morning. Start her day off in a romantic way.

104. Have her linen hankies monogrammed with your initials and hers.

105.   Give your lover hints on what is important to you in the romance department.

106.   Make the first move! Don't let pride stand in your way.

107.   Swallow your pride after an argument (just this once).

108.   Steal a kiss.

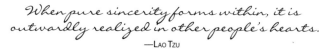
When pure sincerity forms within, it is outwardly realized in other people's hearts.
—Lao Tzu

109.   Change colognes to fit your moods and your romantic feelings. Be sure to wear a fragrance that is pleasing to your mate.

110.   Lower his heart rate by cutting back on his caffeine intake. You, not his soft drink, should be the stimulant for his heart. Help him to take good care of his health.

111.   Sign your Christmas cards from the two of you.

112.   Serve the first cup of morning coffee in a photo mug showing the two of you. It is a great way to start off the day.

113.   Be your mate's secret Santa. Put some magic into his holiday.

114.   Remember that men may be from Mars and women may be from Venus, but we all live together on planet Earth. Everyone just wants to be loved and appreciated. Don't make matters of the heart too complicated!

115.   Act like newlyweds even if you have been together for fifty years!

116.   Serve cheesecake with raspberries for dinner and top it off with a champagne toast.

117.   At the start of each new season, give a piece of trendy jewelry.

118.   Treat yourself with self-respect and you will be sexier, happier, and more attractive to your mate.

119.   Unromantic words to avoid:
✦ Nice   ✦ Fine   ✦ Pleasant   ✦ Okay

Use passionate words to be romantic!

120. Start a "dateograph" book. After every date, write a little something about the evening or your feelings about your lover.

121. Give her a family heirloom:
    ✦ Grandmother's engagement ring
    ✦ Great-aunt's cameo
    ✦ Mother's pearls
    ✦ Fine china
    ✦ Sterling flatware
    ✦ Antique teddy bear

122. Give him a family heirloom:
    ✦ Grandfather's pocket watch
    ✦ Father's family crest ring
    ✦ Uncle's stickpin
    ✦ Grandfather's cuff links

123. For women only: Refrain from male-bashing.

124. Try to win your mate's love and affection all over again.

125. Get a joint his-her makeover.

126. Set up a trust fund for your love.

127. Talk about each other's definition of love. Make sure that you understand your mate's point of view. Make sure that he or she understands yours.

128. Write down two good things about your mate every week for an entire year.

129. Log on to eBay and purchase a fun gift for your mate at a great price. You can find just about anything that your mate would ever want there.

130. Learn the fine art of negotiation. This is key for a long-lasting romance.

131. Take long walks together on a regular basis.

132. Share a bottle of wine from the year in which you first met.

133. Know that the busier you are, the more you will need to schedule romantic time together.

134. Act on your romantic whims. The more you indulge your whims, the more romance will appear in your relationship.

135. Snuggle during major thunderstorms. Put the electricity that is in the air to good use.

136. Popular pet names to consider:
    ✦ Honey   ✦ Cookie   ✦ Schmoopie
    ✦ Baby   ✦ Cupcake   ✦ Sweetheart

Memories of the past strengthen love.
—FINLEY EAGLE

137. Loan her your shirts and sweaters (especially letter sweaters).

138. Take things slowly; true intimacy develops over time. Be patient.

139. Leave behind a well-hidden token of your love the next time you go on a long business trip.

140. Tonight, switch sides of the bed that you normally sleep on and see what develops.

141. Have a fun, good-natured snowball fight. Remember the fun you had as a kid.

142. Keep a ton of breath mints around your home, office, and car.

143. Hide a piece of good jewelry in a homemade Popsicle treat.

144. For a touch of elegance and romance, give her an engraved sterling silver comb and brush set.

145. Bring home a warm box of Krispy Kreme doughnuts and surprise your mate with them.

146. Give her more than half of your lottery winnings.

147. Five things to tell your mate when the occasion arises:
    ✦ You were right!   ✦ I'd marry you all over again.
    ✦ You can do it.   ✦ Good job!
    ✦ Bravo, bravo!

A man is rich according to what he gives, not what he has.
—Henry Ward Beecher

148.   While on vacation, give each other little gifts. Look for them as you travel.

149.   For your soft-drink-loving mate, replace the Mountain Dew with champagne.

150.   Write a short love poem or both of your initials, or draw a heart, in the icing on a cake.

151.   Place an ad in the newspaper declaring your love (okay, you might not want to use your real names).

152.   Paint your bedroom a deep, rich shade of red or passion pink to liven things up.

153.   Learn to like or at least tolerate your mate's family and friends.

154.   Listen to a romantic book on tape as you fall asleep in each other's arms.

155.   Send a balloon bouquet instead of a get-well plant.

156.   Tell your mate that he or she is sexy and remind yourself that you are sexy, too!

157.   Dance in the pouring rain together on a hot summer night.

158.   Get married. We did—and for what it's worth, this only improved things in the romance department.

159.   Dine late.

160.   Believe that great love stories do not have endings.

161.   During late January and February, shop the stores for romantic gifts to give throughout the year. The stores are jam-packed with them thanks to Valentine's Day.

162.   Bring your love beautiful flowers from your garden. Plant your love's favorites so that you will have them on hand.

163.   Send yellow roses to show that you are friends as well as lovers.

164.   Save all your love letters and cards from your mate. Keep them all together in a special place of honor.

165.   Hide a tiny box of chocolates under his pillow.

166. Ask your friends for their tried and true romantic tips. Remember to only ask those who are happy in their love lives.

167. Hide gift certificates from her favorite salon around the house for:
    ✦ Hairstyling
    ✦ Facial
    ✦ Manicure
    ✦ Pedicure
    ✦ Massage
    ✦ Personal trainer
    ✦ Stylist

168. Create your own holiday for two. If it works for both of you, why not campaign to make it a national holiday for the rest of us romantics?

169. Sweep your mate off her feet. Buy an electronic foot massager to soothe her tired feet.

170. Feed each other dinner for a little touch of romance tonight.

171. Place a lock on your bedroom door to keep the little ones out, not to keep your mate in.

ROMANTIC RULE #2
Make sure that you truly love and appreciate yourself first. You can't truly love anyone else if you don't have healthy self-esteem.

172. Save a bottle of champagne for a rainy day or for making up after a big fight.

173. When you get a bonus at work, splurge on a gift for your significant other. Or treat yourself and your mate to a fabulous dream date.

174. Tell your mate often that you love him. We all need to hear those words often.

175. Plan to spend every Valentine's Day together till the end of time.

176. Give a CD of Andrew Lloyd Webber's most romantic songs. It is corny, but so nice. Remember to write a little note to go along with the gift.

One of the hardest things in life is having words in your heart that you can't utter.
—James Earl Jones

177. Have a Spouse/Significant Other Appreciation Day.

178. Give her a fabulous foot massage after her day at the shopping mall.

179. Announce your feelings for your sweetie over a public address system in a public place.

180. Wear silk undergarments. You will feel and look sexy.

181. Kiss tenderly and slowly. This may be an art form that you need to practice.

182. Nibble on his ear. Nibble on his other ear.

183. Give her a beautiful gold heart pendant. Place your picture inside it.

184. Have a caricature picture made of the two of you by a well-known artist.

185. Only give sincere compliments. Be sure to give lots of compliments.

186. Place heart-shaped sachets in her lingerie drawers or luggage.

187. Open your heart and soul to your lover. Don't hold back. Take a chance on love.

188. Hum "your song" on your way to pick up your love. It will make you feel romantic.

189. Leave work early and arrange a clandestine meeting with your honey.

190. When you can't afford a dream getaway, rent videos of your ideal destination and enjoy a movie version of your romantic trip.

> *The quickest way to go broke is to start loving beyond your means.*
> —Author Unknown

191. Give each other lots of back rubs during stressful times. Purchase a hand-held massager to help you be the best massage therapist in town.

192. When your mate takes your hand, squeeze his to let him know that you are glad to be holding hands with him.

193. Forgive and forget. Grudge-holding is not a romantic gesture.

194. Always, always, keep your promises to your love. Great romances are built on trust.

195. Consider taking his name when you marry. More than 90 percent of women do take their husband's name.

196. Stop your family and friends from meddling in your relationship.

197. Try some PDA (public display of affection) today. Show the whole world how you feel.

198. Spritz your home and car with scents that your mate loves.

199. Attend a church service together and hold hands throughout the service.

200. Make a videotape of yourself reading a love poem or singing a love song for your sweetie.

201. When your partner gives you a gift, be sure to use it right away and to use it often. Let your mate know that you think it is fabulous. Show your appreciation.

202. Place heart-shaped doilies under your breakfast muffins.

203. Set up a personal foundation in honor of your loved one. You can start with an endowment of as little as $5,000. Call the Council on Foundations at 202-467-0427.

204. Tease your partner lovingly and gently.

205. Prepare a Christmas stocking for your lover.

206. Know the keys of romance:
      ✦ Love   ✦ Spontaneity
      ✦ Respect   ✦ Sense of fun
      ✦ Sense of humor   ✦ Wanting to please your love
      ✦ Sense of adventure

207. Refer to your wife as your bride.

208. Send a variety of greeting cards, including homemade ones.

209. Celebrate Sweetest Day in October.

210. Learn to say "I'm sorry." Those two words can make a huge difference in the quality of your relationship.

211. Surprise your love in little and in extravagant ways.

212. Place fresh flowers in the refrigerator for her to find after a boring trip to the grocery store.

213. Have a romantic motto that the two of you share and live by, such as:
    - ✦ "Love makes the world go around."
    - ✦ "Two's better than one."
    - ✦ "All the world loves a lover."

It takes two grownups to make a marriage.
—Frances Puzio

214. Ask your mate to name his favorite movie love scene and try to re-create it.

215. Take him out for a change. Sweep him off of his feet.

216. Spoil her silly for an entire week or month. Okay, even a day would be nice!

217. Leave a cute romantic message on his answering machine.

218. Unless she requests one, never, ever, give a cubic zirconia instead of a diamond.

219. Instead of sending fresh flowers, send a silk bouquet and make the romance last even longer.

220. On a beautiful day, stroll hand-in-hand during a nature walk.

221. Instead of staying at major motel chains when you travel, try a bed-and-breakfast or a small country inn for a nice change and lots of romantic ambiance.

222. Tonight, prepare dinner together. It can be lots of fun and very romantic.

223. Hunt for romantic settings such as:
     ✦ Beaches   ✦ Lakes   ✦ Gardens   ✦ Mountains

224. Exchange a tiny remembrance gift at least every month or so.

225. Place confetti in your gift bags, boxes, and greeting cards.

226. Call your significant other and play a tape of "your song" in the background while you chat. Or tape yourself singing it and play it the next time you get together.

227. Hire a caterer to prepare a small feast for two or just to cook dinner once a month.

228. Share your dreams with each other.

229. Install an intercom system in your home so that the two of you can always stay in touch even when you aren't in the same room with one another.

230. Save all the green M&Ms for your love.

231. Give a tape of wedding music for an anniversary present.

232. Hold hands during the next wedding ceremony you attend.

233. Great places to hide love notes:
     ✦ In the book he or she is reading
     ✦ In the cookie jar
     ✦ Under her pillow
     ✦ Folded in his bath towel
     ✦ In pockets
     ✦ In a box of his favorite junk food
     ✦ In storage boxes
     ✦ In his car
     ✦ In her briefcase

234. Be her coach at Lamaze classes. Attend all classes with her. Take her to all of her doctor appointments.

235. Leave your radio tuned to a classical music station.

236. Place a small bouquet of violets on her pillow.

237. Most lovers serve breakfast in bed—why not try dinner in bed?

238. Always keep a current picture of your love on your nightstand.

239. Reminisce often about your wonderful times together.

240. Save newspapers from your anniversaries. Years from now, you'll enjoy reading them together.

241. Be a little outrageous in the romance department from time to time. Surprises work wonders!

242. Give meaningful gifts to your love. Take your time picking out your gifts. Never ever be a last-minute shopper.

243. Exercise together. That will make it more enjoyable and you can both get into shape.

244. On a beautiful spring day, rent a bicycle built for two.

245. Talk to each other about sex. Don't be embarrassed. You need to understand each other's viewpoints clearly.

246. Look for restaurants that have beautiful views. Sit by the windows, or in nice weather try sitting outside.

247. Make a trip to the card store at least once a month. Stock up on the upcoming holiday cards and all kinds of romantic "thinking of you" cards.

248. Go on a moonlit picnic instead of the usual daytime version. Nighttime is much more romantic.

249. Have an instant new chair. Sit in his lap.

250. Write a little message with lipstick on the bathroom mirror.

251. Place romantic stickers on all the love notes, date invitations, and letters that you send.

252. Instead of sending one bouquet, why not send two or three and really express your feelings in a wonderful manner?

253. Write silly, lovey-dovey messages in her fashion magazines or in his sports magazines.

Flattery—telling your lover exactly what he thinks of himself.
—Unknown

254. For a little touch of yuppie romance, purchase matching Coach briefcases.

255. For men only: Put her before your:
     - ✦ Career/job   ✦ Sports
     - ✦ Buddies   ✦ Hobbies

256. For women only: Put him before your:
     - ✦ Career/job   ✦ Mother   ✦ Pets
     - ✦ Children   ✦ Girlfriends

257. Place a menu from a fabulous restaurant under his windshield wiper with a note to meet you there for dinner.

258. Share one meal together every single day.

259. Give him a sexy wakeup call when he is out of town on business.

260. When someone gives you a gift, share it with your mate when it is appropriate to do so.

261. Give him or her "the look" from across a crowded room.

262. Keep your lips soft, your breath fresh, and your teeth whitened to be irresistibly kissable.

263. Take a drive or stroll down Lover's Lane.

264. Ask your mate out for a date a year in advance, just to show that you plan on being together. Plan a great New Year's Eve or Valentine's Day date.

265. Inscribe any rings that you give with a romantic saying. Remember to allow extra time to get this done if you need it for a special occasion.

266. Give him a facial at home or send him to a coed spa.

267. To set a romantic mood, serve a fine wine with dinner tonight.

268. Travel around the world together.

269. Walk your dog together and use the time to really talk and to catch each other up on your daily lives.

270. Give him a severe case of goosebumps.

271. At your next dinner party, use place cards. Instead of your lover's name, write "World's Best Mate."

272. Play an adult version of hide-and-seek or tag. Chase each other all over your home.

273. Send your mate a holiday letter (you know, the kind where everyone brags about the past year). Tell your love how fabulous your love life is with him and how happy you are. Be sure to include anecdotes, highlights, and vacation stories.

274. Carry a cellular phone to keep in touch at all times.

275. Just kiss for a whole night.

276. For a shopaholic mate, take her shopping along Bond Street and Piccadilly in London.

277. Stop trying to manipulate your mate. Let go of the need to control. Be carefree.

278. Spend every February 29th together for the rest of your lives.

279. Give him a piece of diamond jewelry for a change. We suggest:
    - ✦ Ring
    - ✦ Cuff links
    - ✦ Watch
    - ✦ Tie tack
    - ✦ Stickpin

280. Share a raft or blanket at the beach on a pretty summer afternoon.

281. Talk out your problems face-to-face. Hold hands.

282. Secretly pay off all his speeding or parking tickets.

283. Make a great screen saver of the two of you on a fun date and have his coworker load it on his computer while he is at lunch.

*The heart is the first
feature of working minds.*
—Frank Lloyd Wright

284. This is a very important key to a great romance and it sounds simple, but you must work at doing it on a regular basis: Have fun together. Plan activities that you both enjoy.

285. Take over for her at home with the children and the chores.

286. Send mistletoe in June. Why kiss just at Christmas?

287. Keep in mind that unexpected gifts are usually the most treasured ones.

288. Go skinny-dipping at midnight.

289. Knit a sweater for him.

290. Be her caddie at her golf tournament and hide little gifts in her golf bag.

291. Place his phone number in the number one spot on your speed dial and make sure he knows that he holds this little place of honor.

292. Cook dinner together using your fireplace.

293. Buy matching T-shirts and wear them when you go on a picnic.

> *One way for a husband to get the last word is to apologize.*
> —Peggy Caroline

294. Give up thinking of romance as something for sissies and wimps. Remember that some of the world's most famous romantics were men.

295. Send a prayer book to your mate when you know that he is going through a rough time. Inscribe the book with a notation stating that you will always love him, no matter what happens.

296. Ask your travel agent to throw together a great last-minute vacation. Or check out the last-minute specials on travel Web sites.

297. Have a florist, a personal shopper, and a travel agent that you can count on to keep your romance running smoothly. Everyone needs a little help from time to time.

298. Keep in mind that moods are contagious. Let's hope your mate catches your romance fever.

299. Wish on a falling star together.

300. Create a fabulous second childhood together where you give each other the love and nurturing that you both missed in your first childhoods.

301. Place your business card in her wallet in case she needs your work number or fax number in an emergency. Write a little note on the card telling her that you will always be there in a jam.

302. Celebrate St. Nicholas night on December 6 by giving your love a small holiday gift or decoration. Let this occasion be a great start to the Christmas season.

303. Call her once a day from the office just to say, "Hi." Give her a buzz when you know it will be a good time for her to chat for a few minutes.

304. When you mow the lawn, design a message in the grass. It helps if you can look down on the grass from a second story.

305. Share anecdotes of your day with each other and be sure to include any romantic feelings that you felt for your mate during the day.

306. Make your relationship a safe, romantic harbor in the storms of your lives.

307. Give every day a festive feeling by placing little party favors at his place setting at dinner. Check out your local card shop or dollar stores for fun little gifts.

308. Curl up under a beautiful Christmas quilt and watch:
     + *It's a Wonderful Life*   + *Scrooge*
     + *Miracle on 34th Street*   + *Elf*
     + *The Grinch That Stole Christmas* + *The Polar Express*

309. Make a love note from old candy bar wrappers by using the candy bar names to speak of your feelings.

310. Take her to see a production of Rodgers and Hammerstein's *Cinderella*.

311. Always return your lover's calls promptly to show just how much she means to you.

312. Act like kids and have a water fight on a hot summer day.

313. Try looking at your mate with your heart and your soul.

314. On a rainy day, create a travel wish list of all the places that you both want to visit together.

315. Read *2002 Ways to Find, Attract, and Keep a Mate* and concentrate on the parts about keeping your love happy.

316. Have your own special ways of letting each other know when you are "in the mood." Don't tell anyone your secret code.

317. Plant a romantic and beautiful rose garden for her. Bring in fresh roses for her all of the time.

318. Give 150 percent to your mate and your relationship.

319. Add a little excitement to your dates by double-dating with different kinds of people. Just remember always to go out with happy couples.

320. Start a collection of knickknacks or other kinds of memorabilia that you both would enjoy having and collecting.

321. Give your love a sterling silver letter opener to open your love letters.

322. Strive to be a happy couple, not a perfect couple. Be realistic about your romantic expectations.

323. Ask for hugs and kisses instead of material gifts. Your mate will love you for it.

324. Always keep your mate's confidences, no matter how juicy they are.

325. Five things to tell your love on a regular basis:
     + You are wonderful.   + You are amazing.
     + I'll always love you.   + You are my one true love.
     + You are the best.

326. Make the necessary sacrifices for your relationship. Being a true romantic requires putting your mate's needs ahead of your own at times.

The heart that loves is always young.
—Greek proverb

327. On a regular basis, get away together from:
     - ✦ Your job
     - ✦ Your children
     - ✦ The real world
     - ✦ Your in-laws
     - ✦ Household chores and responsibilities

328. Throughout the year, shop for little gifts for your mate to help ensure that you will have lots of "perfect" gifts instead of last-minute leftovers.

329. When it comes to romance, keep in mind that it is better to err on the side of too much instead of too little.

330. Ask, not demand, that your lover make romantic gestures that are important to you. Let her know of your wishes, hopes, needs, and desires.

331. Have a band play "your song" at the next wedding or dance that you attend together. Don't save all of the romance for the newlyweds.

332. When you want to be romantic, refrain from conversations about:
     - ✦ Your work
     - ✦ Your children
     - ✦ World events
     - ✦ Your in-laws
     - ✦ Money
     - ✦ Sad subjects

333. Take walks after midnight.

334. Look up the definition of romance in the dictionary and try to understand all that real romance incorporates.

335. Get new lighting in your dining room so that you have a very soft, romantic atmosphere to dine by.

336. Have a contractor remodel your bedroom and put in a fireplace. They are so romantic.

337. Give her a diamond friendship ring to show her that you think of her as your lover and as your friend.

338. Create your own fortune cookies by inserting personal, romantic fortunes into store-bought fortune cookies.

339. Buy her flowers from a street vendor on your way home from work. Let her know that she is in your thoughts even after a long day at work.

340. Send a bouquet of white roses symbolizing that your love is pure and true.

341. Place a handsome silk tie in his briefcase before he heads off to a big meeting.

342. Get a pretty needlepoint pillow that says "tonight" and place it between the pillows on your bed.

343. Draw a little cartoon expressing your feelings for your mate.

344. Dress up in your best clothing for your next date, or buy a new outfit. Dress to impress!

345. Brush her hair for her at bedtime.

346. Play hooky together from your careers, responsibilities, and the world. A little escape can be very good for your relationship.

347. Make her happy after a long day by preparing a candlelight bubble bath for her.

348. Have you had a major blowup? Try sending a dozen "I'm sorry" cards to your mate's office.

349. Fill her briefcase with love notes. Fill her briefcase with roses. Fill her briefcase with chocolates.

350. Take a vacation day off from work on Sweetest Day to enjoy it with your love or to plan a special celebration when she gets home from work.

351. When you dine out on your mate's birthday, always have a birthday cake brought to your table for dessert.

A smile is not only a woman's best cosmetic, but it likewise serves as a nonverbal compliment to her companion.
—Dr. George W. Crane

352. Send a roll of Life Savers with a note stating that your mate is your real-life lifesaver.

353. Give a gift of eternal value by sharing your faith.

354. Take lots of photographs of you and your mate when you are on vacation and at other times when you are having extraordinary fun together. Let the pictures serve as happy reminders of these special moments together.

355. Keep a journal about your relationship and share all of the good things you write in it with your love.

356. Indulge his sweet tooth with an ice cream cake and be sure to have a sweet message written on top of the cake.

357. Give up watching soap operas on television—they are bad relationship role models. Find some positive role models for your relationship.

358. To put yourselves in a mellow mood, get a CD of environmental sounds.

359. Does your love have the wintertime blues? Head to a warm, sunny place such as:
    ✦ Florida   ✦ Arizona   ✦ Hawaii   ✦ California

    These climates should heal the blahs and warm things up between the two of you.

360. On a cold, dreary night, curl up together and read the works of Henry David Thoreau.

361. Be each other's best friend.

362. Give for the sake of giving. Don't expect anything in exchange for your gifts. That way you will have the spirit of giving like a true romantic.

363. Send him a virtual card to get him thinking about you.

364. Hide a piece of jewelry in a red Jell-O dessert and top it off with whipped cream.

365. Give a gift certificate to a perfume shop when you want to buy a present but feel unsure about what to buy.

366. Enjoy Candlemas Day (February 2) by having candles everywhere in your home.

367. Dye all your Easter eggs red instead of the usual pastel colors for a little touch of romance.

368. Never, ever gossip with your friends about your lover. If he or she finds out, you would be in big trouble.

369. Strive to keep your relationship as tear-free as possible. Love should make you feel good, not sad.

370. Stop saving romance for:
     ✦ Holidays   ✦ Vacations   ✦ Anniversaries

371. Even if she just has a cold, always bring her flowers when she is sick.

372. Throw a coin into a fountain and make a romantic wish together.

373. Dress in a style that will be pleasing to your mate (at least once in a blue moon).

374. Plant a beautiful window box outside her bedroom window.

375. Make it a three-day weekend instead of the usual two-day version. Make some great plans with your significant other for great dates.

376. Send her a postcard of the city that you two are going to on your next vacation. Write a great love note on it.

377. When you have absolutely no idea what to give her for a special occasion, take her on a New York City shopping spree to pick out her gifts from you.

378. Close the drapes, pull down the blinds, and put your imaginations to work.

379. Become parents of a different kind together by adopting a pet from an animal shelter. Or, if you know that she wants a pet, give a gift certificate from an animal shelter for a special occasion.

380. Give her a good luck charm to carry on days when she is feeling a little down on her luck. Remember to give her a kiss for luck, too.

381. Always follow your heart, but use your head.

382. Keep in mind that with arguments there are always three sides to the story:
     ✦ Yours   ✦ Your partner's   ✦ The facts

     Fight the fair fight.

383. Discover paradise hand-in-hand. Try to figure out what your mate's idea of paradise really is.

384. Never overschedule your couple time. You need time for spur-of-the-moment romance.

385. If you need a little help writing love letters, pick up a copy of Reader's Digest's *The Illustrated Reverse Dictionary*. It allows you to start with an idea and then leads you to words with that specific meaning.

386. Before your next getaway, send off for luggage tags and have your and your mate's pet names for each other put on the tags.

387. Want to feel like young lovers again? Try a getaway to Disneyland or Disney World. Plan to stay in the honeymoon suites at the resort.

388. Are you stuck in a romantic rut? Want to get his heart pounding wildly? Try:
     ✦ Parasailing   ✦ Sky diving
     ✦ White-water rafting   ✦ A roller coaster ride

     A little adrenaline goes a long way toward promoting passion.

389. Send a May Day bouquet on May 1.

390. Take an old-fashioned Sunday afternoon drive to a scenic spot and enjoy this time to simply be together. Stop for a late lunch at an out-of-the-way inn.

*A variety of nothing is better
than a monotony of something.*
—Jean Paul Richter

391. Use cute magnets to attach romantic cartoons and mementos to your refrigerator door. Put up a couple of great photos of the two of you, too.

392. Give him a personalized license plate for his new car. Contact the Bureau of Motor Vehicles to determine what initials are available.

393. Send a musical greeting card to your love. If possible, send one that plays "your song."

394. Buy your mate a fabulous new jewelry wardrobe and, for good measure, throw in a lovely jewelry box.

395. Work at keeping your love always growing and changing for the better.

396. Listen to Mozart tonight instead of hard rock.

397. Try to keep discovering the hidden little passions, likes, and dislikes of your mate.

398. Stop yourselves from going to bed angry at each other. Kiss and make up. Talk it out. Pray together. Agree to disagree if you must, but never go to bed mad.

399. During difficult relationship times, try to remember why the two of you got together in the first place.

ROMANTIC RULE #3
Understand that true romance takes effort and hard work at times.

400. Only in an emergency—I repeat, only in an emergency—should you break a date.

401. Are you thinking about him? Pick up the phone and tell him!

402. Seduce your mate tonight. Seduce your mate this afternoon. Why wait?

403. If you want passion to be a part of your love life, try being passionate.

404. Keep both of your passports current so that you can take off on a moment's notice to an exotic getaway.

405. Sing a duet with your love. You don't have to be great singers to have fun singing together.

406. Place your jacket around her shoulders on a cool evening. Be an old-fashioned gentleman when the occasion arises.

407. Hold a private conversation between the two of you in absolute darkness.

408. Three little keys to romance:
   ✦ Secrets   ✦ Sexiness   ✦ Silliness

409. Hold her when she cries and wants to be comforted. Always have a shoulder to spare for her tears.

The only lasting beauty
is the beauty of the heart.
—Rumi

410. Throw a party and invite all the members of your wedding party. Don't wait for your anniversary.

411. Take good care of him when he is sick—yes, even if he is a big baby.

412. Learn the knack of being impractical. Romance isn't practical.

413. Tell your mate what turns you on. Remember, she can't read your mind.

414. Wrap a love note around his medicine bottle when he is sick.

415. When you write a love letter, try to make it thought-provoking, romantic, memorable, timely, and even a bit haunting.

416. If he suffers from a case of "blue Mondays," send him a cheer-up card at work each Monday.

417. Search out romantic settings in your area, such as
   ✦ Art galleries   ✦ Scenic drives
   ✦ Quaint cafés   ✦ The seashore
   ✦ Museum gardens   ✦ Mountaintops

418. Whenever you vacation, always make it a point to dine at a fabulous, memorable restaurant. When you get home from your trip, you will be glad that you have those special memories.

419. Give up trying to change your mate and start changing yourself. It is almost impossible to change another.

420. Make a wreath out of red M&Ms for Valentine's Day. (Call the company at 800-627-7852 for instructions.)

421. Give her a new version of her favorite childhood toy. Bring a smile to her face and show her just how thoughtful you really are.

422. Think of your love as a special gift from God. After all, it really is!

423. When you both need some rest, buy matching satin eye masks.

424. On a lovely summer night, sleep on your screened-in porch together. Enjoy the fresh air and the sounds of the night.

425. If she won't tell you what she wants for Christmas, take her to visit Santa. Then ask the bearded gentleman what she said.

426. Carry a beeper so that you can always be in touch with each other.

427. Spend the holidays together in exotic locations.

428. Always treat your partner with respect. There are no exceptions here!

429. If he hates to shop for clothes, do it for him or send him a subscription to several men's clothing catalogs.

430. Send a love letter wrapped in a huge box and have it delivered by registered mail to her office.

431. Rent a convertible for your next date on a pretty day.

432. Fill every one of her shoeboxes with little Valentines.

433. Buy her anything that is connected with feathers for a little touch of the exotic:
     + A boa   + Slippers   + A feather pen

434. For men only: Read *The Secret Language of Women* by Sherrie Weaver for a fun, offbeat guide to the gentler sex.

435. Love so you don't have any regrets. Live so you don't have any regrets.

436. Get matching vanity license plates for your cars.

437. Meditate together.

438. The number one relationship killer: taking each other for granted.

439. The number two relationship killer: putting up walls.

440. The number three relationship killer: not expressing your true feelings.

441. The number four relationship killer: being complacent.

442. Get out your parents' or grandparents' Big Band albums. Make a great tape of some wonderful dance music. Now, get dancing!

443. Plan a trip down California's Highway 1 for the most picturesque trip of your life.

444. Court each other on a daily basis. Little things go a really long way in the romance department.

445. Keep your teasing to fun topics (that means fun for both of you).

> *Men always want to be a woman's first love—women like to be a man's last romance.*
> —Oscar Wilde

446. How about spending the evening going parking at a teenage make-out spot? Don't let your kids find out!

447. Thrill your sweetie with a fabulous surprise trip to Paris for the two of you.

448. Hire a professional songwriter to write a song for your love. Hire a band to perform it.

449. Make a donation to your mate's favorite charity instead of giving a gift.

450. Always celebrate your lover's birthday (even the ones that your lover would rather forget).

451. When she suggests that you save money by not exchanging gifts for a special occasion, refuse! Always give her a gift.

452. Place the flowers he sends you in a place of importance in your home and where he will be sure to see them.

453. Keep in mind that romantic gestures always have a snowball effect on a relationship. They create more romance!

454. Rules for fabulous, romantic gift giving:
     ✦ Make it expensive or extravagant.
     ✦ Be sure the gift will be highly desired.
     ✦ Give it at an unexpected time.
     ✦ Present it in an unusual manner.
     ✦ Don't let it be practical in any way, shape, or manner.
     ✦ Attach a romantic sentiment to it.

455. Both of you should read the current bestsellers on relationships and then discuss them.

456. Attend a romance workshop together. Many churches are now offering relationship retreats, so check them out for a big help in improving the quality of your relationship.

457. Just for the fun of it, place a silk nightie in her briefcase so that she'll have some pleasant thoughts of you when she gets to her office.

458. Buy her a new outfit for your next evening out on the town. If you need some help, ask a friend or her mom to go along with you on your shopping trip.

459. Make a toast to your mate at your next party. Make it a romantic one that she will remember for years to come and that her friends will be talking about with her on their next get-together.

460. Visit all your friends and family who live in exciting locations for a low-cost getaway.

461. Stop putting off being romantic! Bring your mate flowers and candy tonight!

462. Stock up on your love's favorite junk food so that being with you will be even nicer.

463. Splurge on her dream car. How about a BMW or a Cadillac? For him, how about a Corvette or a Mercedes?

464. For a small touch of romance, sleep on satin sheets.

Oh, be swift to love, make haste to be kind.
—Henri-Frederic Amiel

465. Focus on all the good things about your mate. It improves the quality of your relationship and it is easy to do.

466. Make a lengthy list of all the blessings that are a part of your relationship. Start adding to the list on each anniversary and holiday.

467. Kiss at stop signs.

468. Kiss at red lights.

469. Kiss at railroad crossings when you must wait for a long time.

470. Frame the lyrics to a beautiful love song and give them to your love.

471. When she travels by air, always take her to the airport. When she comes back home, pick her up.

472. Decorate your love's Christmas gifts with:
    + Mistletoe   + Special ornaments
    + Candy canes   + Chocolate Santa

    Remember that the presentation of a gift is almost as important as the gift itself.

473. Meet your lover at the door wearing a costume to liven things up just a bit.

474. Leave a trail of small chocolates for your love to follow and to find you waiting for him.

475. Drop the daily grind in favor of romance. Be a spur-of-the-moment kind of lover.

476. Never hold back when you are expressing your love for your mate.

477. Meet for an afternoon tea party at a grand hotel.

478. Ask your mate to give you a list of his favorite love songs. Put the list to good use.

479. Perfume all your love letters or write on scented stationery.

480. Get home earlier than your mate and meet her at the front door with a teddy bear and flowers.

481. Go fruity! Stop by a bath shop and pick up little bottles of fruit-scented gels and lotions for your love.

482. On evenings when you are both too busy to do the dishes, furnish beautiful paper plates to use at the dinner table.

483. Validate your lover's feelings. Everyone wants and needs to feel understood.

484. Make a wise investment in the local job market and hire a sitter for your children so that you two can enjoy a night out. Have a weekly date night away from your children. It is a good example for the kids to see.

485. Instead of going out, hire a sitter to entertain your children while the two of you enjoy an evening at home.

486. Start a little collection of all kinds of candles:
     ✦ Tapers   ✦ Votive   ✦ Holiday

487. Place a tin of gourmet cookies in his briefcase before his next business trip.

488. Place a "Do not disturb" sign on your office door when your lover visits.

489. Have a little romantic fun of another kind. Play Cupid for another couple.

490. Kiss him more often. Spoon every night.

491. Wash her hair in rainwater.

492. Always take her telephone calls. Show her that she is important to you.

493. Carry her over all hotel thresholds. Treat her like a bride.

494. Have personalized labels made for his liqueur or wine bottles. Try to add a touch of romance to them, such as a small heart in one corner.

495. Buy a mood-music CD. They are inexpensive and available at most discount stores and record shops.

496. Give her a gift certificate for maid service. We guarantee she'll like this one!

497. Present your mate with a blue ribbon for being the world's best lover.

498. Spend an evening together watching your old home movies to recapture the romance of earlier times.

499. Wrap her gifts in gifts. Use:
- ✦ Scarves
- ✦ Quilts
- ✦ Tablecloths
- ✦ Shawls
- ✦ Placemats

500. Ask her friends what it would really take to impress her. Then do it!

501. Kiss, kiss, kiss. Here is a list of reasons to kiss, as if you need any!
- ✦ Kiss hello
- ✦ Kiss with sexual innuendo
- ✦ Kiss of gratitude
- ✦ Kiss—just because!

502. E-mail him a list of five unusual date ideas to stir things up for the weekend ahead.

503. Cover a wall with photographs of the two of you. Use thumb-tacks on a cork base to hang the pictures.

504. Can't get away for the weekend? Take a fun day trip. A small dose of romance is better than no romance at all.

CYNDI'S PICKS FOR BEST/CLASSIC LOVE SONGS:

"Someone to Watch Over Me" – Linda Ronstadt

"Every Time I Close My Eyes" – Babyface

"I Knew I Loved You Before I Met You" – Savage Garden

"Chances Are" – Johnny Mathis

"Love Me Tender" – Elvis

"Breathe" – Faith Hill

"Un-break My Heart" – Toni Braxton

"Can't Help Falling in Love" – Elvis

"The Dance" – Garth Brooks

"Unforgettable" – Nat King Cole

505. Re-create your first meeting (even if it means a pilgrimage across the country) on the anniversary of your first meeting.

506. For a first-class night's sleep, order Egyptian cotton sheets for you and your love to enjoy.

507. Have a beautiful tea set hand-painted for your tea-loving mate.

508. Create a home spa for the two of you to enjoy.

509. Throw the PERFECT party in honor of your mate. Hire a party planner. Get your friends to help.

510. Dress up her beloved pooch for the holidays. Go one step further and have the pooch bring her a gift. Be sure that the costume is safe and comfortable for Fido.

511. Pick up silly souvenirs of your travels together. It will make for some happy reminders after you've been home for a bit.

512. Always call when you tell your mate that you are going to call.

513. Treat her like a queen. Treat him like a king. Okay, for at least a day!

514. Put a little touch of romance in the air—buy a bubble machine.

515. Fix a basket of homemade goodies for your significant other.

516. Memorize your favorite love poem.

517. Give a gift certificate from a lawn and garden center to your nature-loving mate.

518. For your anniversary, give her a fabulous new wedding band. Have your jeweler create one especially for her.

519. Try a touch of sensible romance. Give a month's or a year's worth of:
      ✦ Lunches   ✦ Subway tokens   ✦ Parking

520. Ask your mate for his or her definition of commitment. To be a great couple, both of you must have the same idea of commitment.

521. Escape from the pressures of modern civilization with your mate. Relax. Unwind.

522. Give your mate loads of attention and affection. She will love you for it.

523. Celebrate the idea of Valentine's Day throughout the year. Think about romance every single day.

524. Give up nagging your mate. Just remember that nagging is the most unromantic thing that you can do.

525. Come home early from work to take her to a romantic matinee.

526. Send a huge basket of nuts to her at the office with a note saying that you are nuts for her.

527. Have a special fragrance created just for her. Or surprise her with a trip to France to tour a perfume factory.

528. Send a coupon to celebrate Valentine's Day all over again.

529. Create your own book of great romantic quotations and give it to your love on a special anniversary.

530. When you build your first home, write both of your initials in the freshly poured concrete driveway or patio. Carve your initials on your deck.

531. When he gets a raise or promotion, send him a split of champagne at the office to enjoy at lunch.

532. When you are planning a romantic dinner, use your sense of smell, touch, taste, sight, and sound to create an unforgettable evening.

533. Purchase a set of brightly colored markers to make your love notes a work of art.

534. In the evenings, always keep your lights turned down low to set a romantic mood.

535. If he brown-bags his lunches, put yummy gourmet treats in his sack. Be sure to include a note from you.

536. Place gifts in heart shaped boxes for beautiful gift giving.

537. Trade love stories with other romantics. You can't ever have too much romance in your life. Plus, you might get some great ideas that you can put to good use in the future.

538. Write a love note in chalk on her sidewalk or driveway.

539. Throw at least one party together a year. Turn it into an affair that everyone wants to be invited to because it is so special.

540. Take the romantic lead in your relationship. Be assertive. Be creative.

541. For men only, here is a little tip: Many women find talking to be the best type of foreplay.

542. Place oversize pillows in front of your fireplace for great late-night snuggle sessions.

543. When it comes to dating, be a good sport. Do what your mate wants to do without complaint.

544. Tell her that it is your turn to:
    + Do the dishes   + Clean the house
    + Change the baby   + Drive the kids to school

    These statements will be beautiful music to her ears.

545. Sign your letters and cards with X's and O's (kisses and hugs).

546. Always compliment the cook. Always kiss the cook.

547. Remember that two can dream bigger than one, so get your mate involved in planning:
    + Romantic gestures   + Getaways
    + Vacations   + Holiday celebrations

548. Arrange clandestine meetings with your sweetie all over town.

549. Call to see if your mate needs you to pick up something on your way home from work.

550. Place heart-shaped bookends on his bookshelf for a touch of romance.

551. Go on an old-fashioned romantic fall hayride.

Friendship consists in forgetting what one gives and remembering what one receives.
—Dumas

552. Be the spark in your lover's eyes. Put the spark in your lover's eyes.

553. Escape from your children for a weekend. Get your parents to baby-sit. Treat yourselves and make it a weekend to remember.

554. Fly a heart-shaped kite on windy days and let the whole world know that you are a romantic.

555. Get some ESP going between you and your lover. Spray perfume lightly on your light bulbs.

> *If I create from the heart, nearly everything works, if from the head, almost nothing.*
>
> —Marc Chagall

556. Share a bottle of unisex cologne that you both love.

557. Order a romantic dress or accessory for her from a mail order catalog.

558. Keep the celebration going by giving another present on the day after your mate's birthday. Surprise her with a gift every month for a year on the date of her birthday.

559. Go all out for romance by building a heart-shaped deck or patio.

560. Stop taking phone calls from your ex. No good ever comes from hanging on to an old flame.

561. Wait for her under the mistletoe and remember to never kiss anyone but your mate under the mistletoe.

562. Treat her to a gorgeous evening gown.

563. Send her an old-fashioned homecoming corsage before the big game.

564. When you aren't ready to use the word "love," try one of these:
      - Devotion
      - Respect
      - Affection
      - Regard
      - Warmth

565. Try to be enchanting on your next date. Rent a yacht for a day with a group of your couple friends. Bring along your sense of adventure and of romance.

566. Invent your own little reasons to celebrate together.

567. Always remain true to your mate.

568. Use fresh flowers as you would use bows on presents.

569. For a change of routine in your kiss repertoire, try kissing your mate's neck, chin, forehead, or eyelids.

570. Always open car doors for her.

571. Send a cactus instead of the usual type of potted plant. Include a note saying that you are stuck on him.

572. Tint your popcorn red for your Valentine's Day movie date.

ROMANTIC RULE #4
Keep in mind that you will have emotional highs and lows even in the best of relationships. Great romantics learn how to go with the flow and to ease things back into the best of times.

573. Send a rosemary plant with a note saying that you will always remember:
      + Your mate   + Your time together
      + Last night   + Your wedding day

574. Celebrate the Summer Solstice (June 21) by going out to a summer festival or just spending time together.

575. Host a Valentine's Day tea in honor of your mate. Invite all of her closest girlfriends.

576. Ask your love to give you a list of her favorite meals and desserts. Next, get busy learning how to cook them. Ask her mom for help.

577. Send your mate to a wonderful spa for a day, weekend, or week of pampering when you feel that she needs some extra TLC.

578. Fill his car with pink and red balloons. Tape a love letter to the dashboard.

579. To be a successful romantic, pay attention to the tiniest details when planning dates, vacations, and gift buying.

580. Keep in mind that the most romantic people are:
     - ✦ Playful
     - ✦ Lighthearted
     - ✦ Whimsical
     - ✦ Tenderhearted

581. Brighten your love's day by sending flowers for no reason. We guarantee that it will do the trick.

582. Give him a leather Bible with your names and wedding date inscribed on the cover.

583. Spend the night in a fabulous hotel in your own city for a romantic but easy getaway.

584. Wink at each other often.

585. Blow kisses to each other from across a crowded room.

586. Give two to five hugs to each other every single day—no exceptions, please.

587. Buy him a jersey of his favorite team.

588. Plan a romantic comedy marathon weekend and rent all of the most popular videos to watch together.
     - ✦ Plan your favorite pastimes.
     - ✦ Dine at your favorite restaurant.
     - ✦ Listen to romantic music.
     - ✦ Give a little gift to each other.

589. Call every time you are running late. Never make your mate worry.

590. Take an afternoon nap together before a big night out on the town. Being tired is very unromantic.

591. Choose the most beautiful engagement ring that you can afford. After all, she will have it for the rest of her life.

592. Give your love an old-fashioned friendship ID bracelet for a nostalgic touch of romance.

593. Try to come up with a new romantic idea each week and be sure to put it into practice.

594. Take her mother to lunch, and she and her mom will love you for your kindness.

595. Look to great, happy couples as role models for your relationship.

596. Feeling a little timid? Start small:
    ✦ Place his favorite candy bar under his pillow.
    ✦ Put a romantic CD in her personal CD player.
    ✦ Place a tulip on her pillow.
    ✦ Give a McDonald's gift certificate for breakfast to a mate who never has time to eat in the morning.

597. Set a beautiful table setting for each meal that you share with your mate. Don't save the fine china and silver for company.

598. Can't think of anything romantic to say? Just quote some of the best:
    ✦ William Shakespeare
    ✦ John Keats
    ✦ Elizabeth Barrett Browning

599. Mail a suggestive but cute note to your mate at his office. Be sure to mark it "personal and confidential."

600. Scatter rose petals on your bed tonight.

601. Surprise her by doing a tough chore for her that requires your manly strength.

602. Send a gigantic box of chocolates to your love at the office, where he can share the goodies with his coworkers.

603. Find a fancy alarm clock that will play a sweet tune to wake up your sleepyhead. Or get one that allows you to record a wakeup message.

604. Remodel her office while she is out of town on an extended business trip.

605. When your wife first finds out that she is pregnant, give her a fabulous maternity wardrobe. Give her a lovely piece of jewelry when your child is born.

606. Have all her fine jewelry cleaned for her by a trusted jeweler, and surprise her with a new piece hidden among the cleaned ones.

607. Let your neighbors know that you are one romantic guy by having a heart-shaped pool in your backyard.

608. Place a love note in his wallet.

609. Lie on the summer grass side by side and watch cloud formations. What do you see? Look for hearts and cupids.

610. Ask your love out for Valentine's Day a few months in advance.

611. Buy him a dozen boxes of his favorite Girl Scout cookies. You will even make a scout happy with this one.

612. Plant a Christmas tree in honor of your first Christmas together.

613. The two best gifts for a serious relationship are:
     ✦ Time   ✦ Forgiveness

614. Visit the birthplace of the Bard and enjoy a romantic vacation at the same time. Take him to Stratford-on-Avon, England.

615. At his next big birthday party, stand up and make a major tribute to him.

616. Nurture her spirit by creating beautiful surroundings for her. Clean out the clutter. Hire a decorator.

617. Give a basket of fresh handpicked blueberries, strawberries, or blackberries for a little summertime gift.

He who makes a romantic gesture should never remember it and he who receives one should never forget it.
—**Author Unknown**

618. Give a fabulous gift of a bright future by giving your mate a college education.

619. When the two of you leave on a romantic getaway, tuck a little collapsible bag in her suitcase to fill up with mementos of your trip.

620. Send a coupon to go on a date of your mate's choosing.

621. If your mate has trouble remembering dates or runs late, give him a:
     ✦ Watch   ✦ Planner   ✦ Calendar   ✦ Clock

622. At least one night a week go to bed together at 8:30 P.M. Turn off the phone. Turn off the TV.

623. Frolic in a waterfall or stream on a visit to a warm climate.

624. Get a small blackboard for your kitchen and leave little love notes on it.

625. Rent a condo in a fabulously romantic city for a week. How about Venice, Rome, or London?

626. Want to give your mate a needed and much appreciated gift? Try giving her a break!

627. Sit around a campfire and share stories about your past or feelings about your love.

628. Facing a bad day? Pull the covers up over your heads and stay home together.

629. Look at your wedding photographs as if you were seeing them for the first time. Snuggle up and share your memories.

630. Enroll in a flower-arranging class so that you can create your own floral masterpieces.

631. Give yourselves something different to celebrate:
    - Arbor Day
    - Fellowship Day
    - Groundhog Day
    - Loyalty Day
    - Children's Day
    - Poetry Day
    - Old Maid's Day

632. Watch a made-for-television romantic thriller together. Check out the programs on Lifetime.

633. Vow to please your mate and yourself. Martyrs are never good at romance.

634. Whenever you give a gift to your lover, buy the best one that you can reasonably afford.

635. Re-create an old-time dance party from days gone by. Be sure to include lots of songs to slow-dance to in your musical selections.

636. Strive to be interdependent, not codependent. The happiest relationships are the healthiest.

637. How about bringing sweets to your sweet:
     - ✦ Cobblers
     - ✦ Napoleons
     - ✦ Mousses
     - ✦ Cakes
     - ✦ Cookies
     - ✦ Eclairs
     - ✦ Puddings
     - ✦ Pies
     - ✦ Custards
     - ✦ Glacés

638. Share all your financial assets. Yes, we said all your assets.

639. Dress up in a fun costume to cook a holiday meal for her. Be:
     - ✦ Santa
     - ✦ Easter Bunny
     - ✦ Cupid

640. Surprise your mate by taking a chance on romance on Chance Day (August 7).

641. Give your sweetie some prepaid phone cards when she leaves on a business trip so that she can easily keep in touch with you.

642. Believe that you are very lovable and you will be.

643. Run a bath for her after a hard day. Light a few candles and play some soft music. Warm up her towels with a new towel warmer.

644. At night, share your pillow with your lover.

645. When you are at the beach, slip away from your mate and bury a small gift in the sand. Then give him a shovel and a map to find his buried treasure.

646. When her car is in the repair shop, provide your own personal taxi service for her. At the end of the day present her with your bill and ask her to pay it in kisses.

647. Before you retire to the bedroom for the night, lightly spray it with rose or gardenia air fragrance.

648. Give big bear hugs to your mate. Be the last one to let go.

649. Top off your romantic dinners at home with a piece of fine chocolate candy. Feed it to your mate.

Bonds of matrimony: worthless unless the interest is kept up.
—Author Unknown

650. Go on a spring break like you did as a teenager, but this time, turn it into a romantic spring break with your partner.

651. Allow your heart to fall deeply, madly, and wildly in love. Stop holding back.

652. When she reads a tragic love story, hand her a beautiful lace hankie.

653. Sign your mate up for a subscription to a romantic book club.

654. Secretly place your picture in her locket.

655. Fluff his pillows for him. Pamper him. Take good care of him.

656. Start a romance club with other people who are true romantics and share your ideas about love, romance, and relationships.

657. Write a fan letter to your mate stating all the reasons that he is special to you. Give the letter lots of thought. Make it one that he will treasure for years to come.

658. Build a fabulous, heart-shaped sandcastle the next time you and your love go to the beach.

659. Make a wish together on a new moon for some great romance to come to you (wish over your left shoulder for best results).

660. Take a romantic ride in the Tunnel of Love at the next carnival you visit.

661. Call your favorite restaurant and order your favorite dinner for carry-out tonight for you and your mate. Why be a slave to the kitchen?

What your heart thinks is great, is great.
The soul's emphasis is always right.
—Ralph Waldo Emerson

662. When your mate gets passed over for a promotion, start a cheer-up campaign to raise his spirits. Help him to keep things in perspective. After all, it isn't the end of the world.

663. Order room service for two and stay in your hotel room instead of venturing out on the town.

664. Dress up in a period costume and cook a meal from an antique cookbook.

665. Reserve the penthouse suite for your next business trip, and take your mate along.

666. Dry some flowers from all the bouquets he sends you to make a beautiful new bouquet that is filled with happy memories.

667. Snuggle under a heavy down comforter so that you'll feel as snug as two bugs in a rug.

668. Bake Valentine cookies together and deliver them to all your couple friends.

669. Spend the day together in your jammies. Relax. Take it easy and pamper each other all day long.

670. Keep a healthy mindset of:
     ✦ Love   ✦ Joy   ✦ Happiness   ✦ Fun

671. Know that a trouble shared is a problem split in half. Help each other as much as you can.

672. Have a fun fight—a food fight in the kitchen.

673. Arrange to meet for a morning coffee break.

674. Give a foreign edition of your mate's favorite magazine, newspaper, or book for a little touch of the exotic.

675. Rent an RV and drive to all the towns and cities that have romantic names or attractions.

676. Buy Band-Aids with hearts all over them to give to your mate when she has a little accident.

677. Give her a new wedding gown for when the two of you renew your vows. Be sure that your vows reflect you and your mate's growth through the years.

678. Try to obtain a foreign language version of "your song."

679. Change the lighting in your bedroom by placing an old-fashioned oil lamp on the nightstand.

680. Give her a matching set of cloth-covered boxes filled with little romantic gifts. Hide the boxes throughout the house.

681. On Memorial Day weekend, sit down together and make a lengthy list of all the fun activities that both of you want to do during the upcoming summer months.

682. Be sure to make your dinner hour together a nice, quiet, calming time in your busy day. Stay away from stressful topics.

683. Create boundaries (not walls) within the relationship to allow for personal freedom.

684. Allow extra time for your lovemaking.

685. Write out a fun contract for a month of great dates. Send it to your mate and have him or her sign it and mail it back to you. Make it official that the two of you are going to have four spectacular dates in the next 30 days.

686. When she falls asleep tonight, tuck her favorite childhood toy in beside her to give her a heartwarming surprise when she awakens in the morning.

687. Make a heart out of brown sugar to top off his bowl of oatmeal (one of the few foods that the American Heart Association recommends for a healthy heart).

688. Get a pair of tropical fish for his office and name them for the two of you.

689. Promise her that she'll never have to be out in the dating world ever again. Keep your promise.

690. Put these attitudes to work in your relationship:
     ✦ Giving   ✦ Sharing   ✦ Caring

691. Buy a pair of his-and-her rockers for your porch or deck, and spend your evenings getting reacquainted.

692. Always lend a helping hand to your mate. Be the first to offer help and support.

A way to the heart is through the ears.
—Katie Hurley

693. Give a set of wind chimes to create a wonderful sound of romance on breezy evenings.

694. For a lovely anniversary gift, have a beautiful oil painting made from your best wedding photograph.

695. Give a mini–back rub to your mate when she is stressed and working late at her desk.

696. Surprise your love by getting one of his love poems to you published in a poetry magazine.

697. Order a cake that says, "I want you" and serve it for dessert on your anniversary.

698. During a thunderstorm, snuggle up and watch the storm together. Bring along snacks, drinks, and your sense of wonder. Tell your mate how much you love him or her.

699. Try a little educational romance by visiting a planetarium and seeing a star show.

700. Send a chocolate kiss to him in the mail after a great date.

701. Realize that forgiveness is the end of an argument.

702. Reward all romantic gestures with words of appreciation, hugs, and kisses.

703. Remember that you keep love by giving it away. Don't be stingy.

704. Affair-proof your marriage by:
    + Laughing together often
    + Making love regularly
    + Sharing your lives with each other
    + Telling each other how you feel about one another

705. Give your mate your frequent flyer miles to use toward a fun getaway.

706. Be daring and parachute together in a double parachute. Plan to meet after the big jump for a celebratory dinner.

707. Arrange for your mate to hear you saying nice things about him or her.

708. To improve the spiritual side of your relationship, attend a couples' Sunday school class.

709. Make some sacrifices for your lover. Start small, but significantly, by giving her more of the closet space.

710. Hide a diamond tennis bracelet in her tennis racket case.

Success in marriage is much more than finding the right person; it is a matter of being the right person.
—B. R. Brickner

711. Give him a set of personalized golf balls with your initials or other romantic symbols of your relationship.

712. Decorate your bedroom with floral garlands instead of bouquets.

713. When you come home from work, before asking, "What's for dinner?" tell your mate that you love her.

714. Never confuse your mate's role in your life with your parents' place in your life.

715. Rub wonderfully scented suntan lotion on her shoulders during a day at the beach. Another case of little things mean a lot!

716. Lavishly entertain his boss, friends, and family. Go all out.

717. After an especially hectic week, spend the weekend reconnecting. Unwind together. Just enjoy hanging out with one another.

718. Give her the American dream—the house with the white picket fence around it.

719. When the telephone just won't do, buy a set of walkie-talkies to keep in touch.

720. Hire a topnotch furniture designer to create a wonderfully romantic bed for the two of you to share.

721. On the first night of summer, give your mate a beautiful set of patio furniture so that the two of you can spend more time under the stars.

722. Never suppress a compliment or a positive statement about your love. No one ever tires of hearing good things about him- or herself or relationships.

723. Make love in an unusual place. Liven things up a bit.

724. Improve your romantic skills by reading a book on flirting.

725. Give tea towels, aprons, or potholders with hearts on them to her when you know that she is going to fix an extra-special meal for you.

726. Dine on heart-shaped dishes (available at most gift shops in early February).

727. Remember her beloved pooch on Valentine's Day with a heart collar or a red collar.

728. Give her a lovely pair of red gloves to keep her ring finger warm.

729. For women only: Give him a week's worth of red gifts, such as:

Sunday	T-shirt
Monday	Muffler
Tuesday	Sweater
Wednesday	Tie
Thursday	Shirt
Friday	Robe
Saturday	Silk boxers

730. For men only: Give her a week's worth of red gifts, such as:

Sunday	Gloves
Monday	Umbrella
Tuesday	Shoes
Wednesday	Handbag
Thursday	Slippers
Friday	Robe
Saturday	Nightgown

731. Pick up some heart-shaped rolls or doughnuts for breakfast.

> *A person's world is only as big as their heart.*
> —Tanya A. Moore

732. Even if you have been married for years, pick her up for your next date. Go to the front door and ring the doorbell. After the date, see her to the front door.

733. Propose on a national talk show.

734. Drink only red drinks on Valentine's Day:
    - ✦ Red wine
    - ✦ Cranberry juice
    - ✦ 7-Up with red food coloring
    - ✦ Cherry wine coolers
    - ✦ Red Kool-Aid
    - ✦ Pink champagne
    - ✦ Pink margaritas

735. Attach a heart banner to your lover's mailbox. Take your time decorating it.

> *There is a wealth of unexpressed love in the world. It is one of the chief causes of sorrow evoked by death; what might have been said or might have been done that never can be said or done.*
> —Arthur Hopkins

736. Make an enemy of your lover's letter carrier by sending hundreds of love notes at one time.

737. Before a trip abroad, hide the appropriate foreign currency in your mate's passport to help in her big shopping spree. Include a chart explaining the exchange rate.

738. Replace all her boring manila files with red, pink, and heart-covered ones to spice up her filing system.

739. Make a slide presentation for your love of all your trips together. Play romantic music in the background. Serve a light, romantic snack.

740. Make your own family heirloom by giving your love a piece of estate jewelry.

741. To keep the flame burning bright, get lots of firewood at the beginning of the winter season. Purchase some fragrant fire starters to get the embers burning.

742. Have a powder room or bedroom mirror etched with:
    - ✦ Both of your initials
    - ✦ Your favorite poem
    - ✦ "Your song"
    - ✦ Your anniversary date

743. Plant flowers, bulbs, or a tree on your anniversary.

744. Make up a secret code and write a love letter to your mate. Let your mate have fun trying to decipher it.

745. Collect all your love letters, love notes, and cards, and have them bound into a leather book.

746. Tonight share a sauna and get all "steamy" together.

747. Turn a picture into a classic treasure by hiring a photographer to take black-and-white photographs of the two of you and then framing the best one in a sterling silver frame.

748. Always see her safely home after a date. Walk her to her door and make sure she gets in safely.

749. Purchase matching Valentine's Day pillowcases and use them throughout the year.

750. Need a little escape, but you don't have time? Have a gourmet picnic on the fire escape of a high-rise building.

751. Spend the night together in a child's tree house, or go to camp together. There are lots of camps springing up all over the country that offer fun vacations for adults who want to be like children again.

752. Give your love a copy of *2002 Things to Do on a Date* and ask her to mark all the ideas that appeal to her.

753. Teach her dog to present her with the flowers you brought home from the florist.

754. Have cocktail napkins printed with:
      + Your anniversary date   + The date that you met
      + Both of your initials   + The date that you proposed
      + Your first date anniversary

      Use them often as happy little reminders of your relationship.

755. Keep in mind that your love will be thrilled (and relieved) when you take the romantic lead. Give him a break.

756. Know that your mate wants you to be romantic.

757. Leave more than one message on her answering machine. Make each message more romantic than the previous one.

758. Use your computer to print up romantic:
      + Coupons   + Cards   + Invitations

759.   Romantic tip: You will change and your mate will change. There-fore, your relationship will change. The trick is to make sure that all the changes are in a positive direction.

760.   Schedule a make-out session for this week. Put it on both of your calendars.

761.   When you feel tongue-tied, let a poem title, song title, or book title express your feelings.

762.   Whenever you travel together, call it a honeymoon.

763.   If you simply can't write a good love letter, get a trusted friend to do it for you. Just be sure to swear your friend to secrecy or your name will be MUD.

764.   Rent a large commercial sign for your love's front yard and put a love note on it.

765.   Figure out how much you normally spend on your hobbies, sports, and personal interests for one month. Take that amount of money and spend it on romantic things instead. We guarantee that it will make a huge difference in your life.

766.   Be very bold—throw a surprise wedding for you and your love.

767.   For a night or a weekend, pretend that you and your significant other are stranded on a deserted island.

768.   Create a romantic flag of your own design and fly it in front of her house.

769.   Start a collection of Department 56 Snow Village houses for her and choose buildings that will hold special meaning for her, such as:
   ✦ The honeymoon hotel   ✦ The wedding chapel

770.   Look for ways to break your "standard date rut." Routines lead to boredom in a relationship. Stir things up. Change your normal routine. Go a bit crazy.

771.   Send her a gorgeous Waterford writing instrument to use in her correspondence with you.

772.   Give her a bride figurine for your anniversary.

773. Sign her up for the bridal registry at her favorite store and give her one of the gifts that she most desires.

774. Create an Easter tree for her with little egg ornaments and use a lovely strand of pearls as a garland on the tree.

775. Always send a greeting card in advance of every holiday so that your love will have longer to enjoy the card.

776. Make the most of being stuck in traffic together. Plan upcoming events. Share stories that you haven't told each other.

777. Right now, make up a list of five little romantic gestures that you can do for your mate in the next few weeks. Yes, you have to do them. Just writing them down is not enough!

778. Exercise your lips—kiss your lover. Say romantic things.

779. When he is putting in too many long hours at the office, send him a vintage bottle of Cognac with a note telling him to come home to unwind.

780. Cover a dartboard with photos of your old lovers. Next, let your mate practice his dart-throwing skills.

781. Spruce up your bedroom. Get a new gorgeous bedspread and drapes.

782. Decorate your bedroom like the honeymoon suite at your favorite hotel.

783. Always kiss and make up after a fight.

784. Here are the keys to handling your differences:
    ✦ Learn from them.   ✦ Embrace them.   ✦ Enjoy them.

785. Before jumping out of bed in the morning, do some stretching exercises together.

786. Close your eyes for 30-second intervals throughout the day and think good things about your mate.

787. Hang a Yuletide kissing ball in your foyer and put it to good use. Pucker up!

788. Looking for the perfect gift for your mate? Put a bow around your neck. Voilà!

789. Fix a delicious, romantic, late-night drink. Make a maple cider toddy:

2	*cups cider (apple works best)*
1 to 2	*tablespoons maple syrup*
¼	*vanilla bean, split*
½	*cinnamon stick (for garnishing)*
6	*allspice berries*
½	*cup brandy*

Combine all ingredients but the brandy. Simmer for 20 to 30 minutes. Strain the liquid. Add the brandy. Serve in front of a roaring fire or in bed.

790. For your pizza-loving mate, order an exotic flavor of pizza and share it under the covers on a cold evening.

791. Be her best cheerleader. When she has a problem, be the type of mate that she wants to go to. Be the type of lover that is always supportive and kind.

792. Give her a catalog and gift certificate from Gump's of San Francisco. The jewelry and gifts are the kind of thing that dreams are made of!

793. Stop believing that romance has to cost you a small fortune. The best things in life are free:

- ✦ Kisses
- ✦ Hugs
- ✦ Whispers of sweet nothings
- ✦ Time

The heart has eyes which the brain knows nothing of.
—Charles H. Perkhurst

794. Do something that she has been bugging you to do, but you haven't done. Be a good sport.

795. Plan a relaxing vacation where you simply stay at home and do nothing, but you do nothing together.

796. When you are out to dinner, tell the waiter that you are on your honeymoon and receive better service and a touch of romance.

797. Become a passionate person, not just about romance but also about every aspect of your life. You will be so much more attractive to your mate.

798. Purchase a color printer for your computer so that you can make banners, invitations, coupons, and cards.

799. Every time you send flowers or bring candy to your mate, make it a different kind. Surprise her with your creativity.

800. Learn the art of just being together in silence. It is a hallmark of all great couples.

801. Fill your bedroom with dozens of fresh flower bouquets.

> *Reprove a mate in secret,*
> *but praise him before others.*
> —Author Unknown

802. Arrange to be the vocalist at a wedding in the near future. Before the ceremony begins, tell your love that, in your heart, you will be singing the song to her.

803. Browse through a beautiful bridal department to feel like a bride all over again and to get yourself in a romantic frame of mind.

804. If you are thinking of buying a diamond engagement or anniversary ring, call De Beers for an informative brochure.

805. Make love at a different time than you have ever loved each other before.

ROMANTIC RULE #5
Being romantic is a learned skill. People aren't born that way.
The great romantics work at it.

806. Send a flower that holds special meaning in the world of flowers. Give your love camellias, which in Victorian days signified beauty. Be sure to tell her their meaning.

807. Crash together after a horrific workweek.

808. Place a tiny yet elegant nosegay at her place setting at dinner tonight.

809. When you know in your heart that you have found your special someone, make a spur-of-the-moment marriage proposal.

810. Take a sunset harbor cruise together. Enjoy this beautifully romantic moment.

811. Serve an appetizer before a romantic meal to give yourselves time to unwind after a busy day.

812. Arrange a second honeymoon at a French or Italian villa. Ask your travel agent for help.

813. Use a zillion candles as a romantic centerpiece. Place them on a long mirror to reflect their beauty.

814. Give an aromatherapy lamp to add wonderful fragrances to your home.

815. Order a zany but romantic Smitten Mitten. It is a double glove so that couples can hold hands but still keep the glove on.

816. Give a gift made out of velvet, such as:
     ✦ Dress   ✦ Robe   ✦ Pillow   ✦ Comforter

817. Send a beautiful antique Valentine's Day card to your lover. Look for some at antique shops and flea markets.

818. Refinish an old steamer trunk and give it to her to use as a hope chest.

819. For an international touch of romance and style, give a box of French or Belgian chocolates.

820. Collect sterling silver heart charms and make a beautiful charm bracelet with them for your love.

821. Believe in love at first sight. Believe in a love affair that never ends!

822. For a Victorian touch of romance, give her pearl:
     ✦ Buttons
     ✦ Comb and brush sets
     ✦ Handled flatware

823.   Send a darling sweet pea bouquet for a midweek pick-me-up.

824.   Make a cassette tape of all the music that was played at your wedding. Play it to bring back wonderful memories.

825.   Place twenty tiny love notes inside her umbrella. Close it very gently. This will shower her with your love the next time it rains.

826.   Present her with an antique dance card before you take her out for an evening of dancing.

827.   Are you having an incredibly busy workday? E-mail your mate instead of phoning her.

828.   Name your home or apartment with the help of your mate. Choose a romantic type of name.

829.   Invite your lover for lunch in the private dining room at your place of employment. Arrange to have a small gift at her place setting.

830.   When your love arrives at the airport from an extended trip, have a band waiting at the gate to play "your song."

831.   Bring exotic, lovely flowers back to your mate when you travel alone.

832.   Before a big date, call your love from your cell phone just to say that you are looking forward to your time together.

833.   Propose all over again. Repeat the proposal down to the smallest of details.

A joyful heart is the inevitable result of a heart burning with love.
—Mother Teresa

834.   Call him from the phone on the airplane when you travel without him, just to let him know that you miss him.

835.   Make an event of dinner by making it a pink/red romance meal:

Use:	Serve:
Red table linens	Cranberries and ham
Pink dishes	Strawberries jubilee
Red and pink centerpiece	Pink champagne

836. Place a new sterling silver bookmark in the most romantic part of the book she is reading for her to find.

837. Give your bride-to-be Martha Stewart's *Weddings* magazine to give her marvelous ideas about planning your big day.

838. The only number you will need when it comes to fine chocolates is 1-800-9-GODIVA.

839. Replace your chrome doorknobs with beautiful floral ones for a lovely touch in the bedroom.

840. Give her a wonderful Limoges collectible, such as a:
     - ✦ Hatpin
     - ✦ Button
     - ✦ Brooch
     - ✦ Lady pin

841. For a getaway that you will never forget, travel to London and stay at one of the wonderfully romantic little hotels.

842. Search through flea markets and antique shops and shows to find a lovely antique silver bride's basket to give to her for your anniversary or wedding gift.

843. Take your lover to one of the most romantic spots in the United States—Nantucket Island. Check with your travel agent for the most romantic inns.

844. Buy her a spectacular bauble from a well-known jeweler like Tiffany's or Harry Winston.

845. Cut a heart on the top of his steak before you throw it on the grill. Carve your initials on a cheesecake dessert.

846. Compose a sonnet about all the time you have spent with your love.

847. Kiss goodnight at the front door (even if you are married).

848. Have a talented dressmaker create a miniature version of her wedding gown and present it to her in a shadow box.

849. Take your wedding picture to your florist and have them copy her bridal bouquet in silk flowers to present to her on your anniversary.

850. Before she arrives at your hotel room, decorate it in a romantic style.

851. Send a bouquet of state flowers from your lover's home state.

There is as much greatness of mind in acknowledging a good turn, as in doing it.
—Seneca

852. To feel like young lovers again, spend the weekend at your old college dorm. Dine at the trendy restaurants. Stroll around campus holding hands. Take in a movie at the student union.

853. When you shop with your mate, remember what he liked. Later, go back and stock up on future gifts for him.

854. Invite your mate to have dinner with you at every romantic restaurant in town. If you live in a large city, prepare yourself for one major dining-out bill on your credit card!

855. Slip into the boardroom where she works before her big presentation, just to wish her good luck and give her a little kiss.

856. Look at your lover through rose-colored glasses.

857. Keep in mind that true romantics never confuse lust with love. They never confuse sex with intimacy.

858. Share the covers. Yes, cover stealing can ruin even the best romantic night together.

859. Always treat her like a lady. Always be a gentleman. Good manners never go out of style.

860. Even if you hate his taste in clothes, give him the freedom to choose without your well-intentioned interference. Guide him gently in matters of personal style.

861. Give a huge box of romantic CDs, movies, and books to a lover who is stuck at home. Gift-wrap each item separately and wrap the outside box.

You have to stay awake to make your dreams come true.
—Author Unknown

862. Take good care of your ladylove while you are out of town, by giving her a gift-wrapped box of self-protection presents:

    ◆ Whistles   ◆ Sting spray
    ◆ Door locks   ◆ Alarms

    Enclose a note stating that you care what happens to her and want her to feel safe and loved.

863. Hire a maid for one day a week or month and spend that time together far away from household chores.

864. When you are going to be out of town on business, send your shopaholic mate to New York City with a friend and have gift certificates set up at some of the wonderful shops along Fifth Avenue and 57th Street. That way she won't miss you as much.

865. As you drive home from work, shift gears in your head from business to romance.

866. For men only: Be sophisticated, be debonair, and imagine that you are the James Bond of romance.

867. Spend this weekend at a secluded hideaway. Yes, we said this weekend. Talk to your travel agent for some great ideas.

868. Give your lover every reason in the world to trust you. Never give any reason for him to doubt you.

869. Romantic words to get into your vocabulary and your thoughts:

    ◆ Boudoir   ◆ Escapes   ◆ Rendezvous
    ◆ Fantasy   ◆ Intimacy   ◆ Monogamy
    ◆ Exotic   ◆ Ardor   ◆ Honeymoons
    ◆ Passion   ◆ Chivalry   ◆ Love

870. Be her earthly rock. Be there in good times and bad.

871. Give your mate lots of quality time. Don't skimp and think that quality makes up for lack of quantity.

872. Give your lover a tube of lip-gloss after a long night of smooching to soothe her tired, chapped lips.

873. When you aren't feeling the least bit romantic, give her a set of Harlequin or Silhouette books for a touch of fictional romance.

874. Put gallantry to the test. Throw your coat down over a puddle to prevent her feet from getting wet.

875. At a large party, spend at least part of the time with your mate. Socialize as a couple.

876. Always treat your mate like a special date.

877. If you want to have a charming getaway, get Country Living travel service to plan it for you, because they have the largest selection of country inns and B&Bs in the United States.

878. Stop by the post office in early February for a selection of boxes, stamps, and cards with a romantic theme. Who would have thought that even Uncle Sam is romantic!

879. Give your love a Victorian-style rocker for nights when the baby can't sleep. Help out when your baby can't sleep.

880. Present your love with tickets inside a beautiful handbag to a spectacular charity event.

881. Give her a gift that will make her the envy of all her friends.

The best and most beautiful things in the world cannot be seen or even touched. They must be felt with the heart.
—Helen Keller

882. Carve a cupid on your Halloween pumpkin instead of a scary face. Carve hearts. Carve your initials. Carve your wedding date.

883. Wrap your presents in such a way that your mate won't be able to guess what is inside the box. Remember, surprises are romantic.

884. Find a hobby or pastime that both of you can share. Try new activities together. Branch out.

885. Grow old together, but always keep getting younger at heart.

886. Ditch your beepers and grab some quality private time together.

887. Talk first to each other about your trouble spots, before going to your in-laws and friends.

888. Always stand up for your mate with your family and friends.

889. Tell her that she is pretty. Women love to hear this!

890. Let bygones be bygones if you want to have a healthy, happy relationship.

891. Serve laughter and love with all your meals. Move your bed. Purchase some new sheets. Shake things up a bit.

892. Throw a surprise anniversary party for your mate.

893. Make a list of all the ways that you and your love can create more intimacy in your relationship.

894. Keep in mind that one major component of a quality relationship is the ability to communicate. Spend time sharing:
    - Thoughts
    - Goals
    - Philosophies
    - Experiences
    - Dreams

895. Fix a bulletin board where you tack mementos of your relationship. Place it where the two of you can see it every day and add more souvenirs of happy events.

896. Play date roulette. Make a list of twenty date ideas and place them in a jar. The next time the two of you are stumped for what to do, pull out a date from the jar and do it.

897. Take good care of your hearts:
    - Don't smoke.
    - Eat right.
    - Stay in love.
    - Exercise.
    - Get checkups.

898. Commission a famous artist to paint her portrait. She will be so flattered.

899. Dance outdoors to the radio or a portable CD player on a beautiful night.

900. When you travel, look for hotels, B&Bs, and inns that have fireplaces in the bedrooms.

901. If your lover loves tea or coffee, go out and buy a dozen new flavors. This will be a nice little breakfast treat. Serve it in a heart-decorated mug.

902. Make a list of the rooms in your home. Now make a list of one item that you can buy for each room that will make it more romantic.

903. For your chocolate-loving mate, create coupons good for fudge, cakes, brownies, and cookies that you will make when he redeems the coupons.

904. Shake things up a bit by:
    ✦ Coloring your hair
    ✦ Wearing a new style of clothing
    ✦ Rearranging the furniture
    ✦ Trying a new activity
    ✦ Going to a new restaurant
    ✦ Inviting a new couple along on your date

There is no instinct like that of the heart.
—Lord Byron

905. Plan activities that give you both a feeling of being connected.

906. Give your love a copy of *Rebecca* by Daphne du Maurier to read. It is a wonderful gothic romance.

907. Stop playing games with each other. Honesty really is the best policy.

908. Check out America Online for lots of shopping and gift-giving ideas.

909. Give her a copy of one of the romantic Disney movies:
    ✦ *Beauty and the Beast*
    ✦ *Snow White*
    ✦ *Cinderella*

    Tell her that she will always be your queen.

910. When you want to play solitaire, play the double version just so you two can still be together.

911. If you are married and going through a bad patch, don't even consider divorce as an option. Remember that you promised for better or worse.

912. Host a dinner for two in a greenhouse when all the flowers are in bloom.

913. Have a quilt made that depicts a scene or saying that holds a special meaning for both of you.

914. When he is sick, fix a basket of:
     - Movies
     - Paperbacks
     - Newspapers
     - Snacks
     - Magazines
     - Favorite CDs

915. When you and your significant other see a movie that she loves and it is based on a book, send a copy of the book as a reminder of the good time that you shared.

916. Take an exotic gondola ride in Venice. Too expensive? How about a canoe ride around a pretty local lake?

917. Place Valentine-style decorations throughout your home on your anniversary. Go all out. Make Cupid jealous.

918. Give a tin filled with heart-shaped cookie cutters.

919. Get matching his-and-her pets. We have male and female golden retrievers.

920. Hold hands while doing scary stuff like riding on a ski lift.

921. Take a train trip together. Plan a trip to an exotic location. Turn it into a grand adventure.

922. Sit in the back row of a movie theater and smooch during the slow parts of the movie.

923. Know the meanings behind the different colors of lingerie:
     - **White:** pure
     - **Pink:** sweet
     - **Red:** sexy
     - **Blue:** serene
     - **Black:** sophisticated

924. Give a big bag of red M&Ms, which stand for romance.

925. Always sign your love letters in red ink.

926. Give a week's worth (seven different kinds) of cologne to your lover.

927. Take her to the spectacular Château Frontenac Hotel in Quebec City.

928. When good things happen for your mate, give him a sincere, loving pat on the back. Be happy for him.

929.   Be sure that he has a red or heart-motif tie to wear on anniversaries, Sweetest Day, and Valentine's Day.

930.   Preserve her wedding gown and veil for your daughter.

931.   Wake him up in the morning with a big kiss. Send him off to sleep at night with an even bigger kiss.

932.   Hold her after a bad dream. Comfort her after a bad dream.

933.   Hide your gifts inside other gifts. Turn your gift giving into an art form.

934.   Give a heart-shaped key chain or other style that has a special meaning for the two of you.

935.   Always tell your lover the whole truth, even if it is painful. Trust is so important!

936.   Start a collection of songs that have the word "Valentine" in them. Play them on Valentine's Day and Sweetest Day.

937.   Never, ever have more than one lover at a time.

938.   Use your lover's name only in good times, not during arguments, so that it will always be music to her ears when you say it.

939.   Take care of your own needs so that you won't be a burden to your lover. Be self-sufficient.

940.   Get him a big-screen television to watch his ball games on and keep him company for the really big games.

941.   Make "happily ever after" your reality. Turn it into a joint life goal.

942.   Break the world record for kissing the longest.

943.   Kiss her twice before you leave for work in the morning.

944.   When you need to put stars in your lover's eyes, give him a telescope to view the galaxy. Hopefully, some of the wonder and romance will rub off on him.

945.   Give her an antique enameled box for a little anniversary gift.

946.   Send a floral wreath instead of flowers. Ask the florist to hang it on her door when it is delivered.

947. Put little romantic requests in his office, home, and briefcase, asking for:

    ✦ Hugs   ✦ Snuggling   ✦ Dates
    ✦ Kisses   ✦ Pillow talk

948. Always pull out her chair for her when she sits down at a table and when she gets up from the table.

The test of a happily married and a wise woman is whether she can say, "I love you" far oftener than she asks, "Do you love me?"
—Dorothy Dayton

949. Place a tin of gourmet treats under the bed for yummy late-night snacks.

950. Literally become her knight in shining armor. Go to a costume shop to rent a suit of armor. Why not ride up to her front door on a white horse while you are at it?

951. Give her sole possession of the remote control for a week and you will see a lot more romantic programming.

952. Fly a flag of his favorite team on the day of an important game. Let him know that you share his enthusiasm.

953. Be the first one to suggest a smart, loving compromise to your problem. Become a peacemaker.

954. Tuck a love note in his PJs. Or treat him to some new jammies for a little midweek surprise.

955. Place a greeting card in his lunch bag.

956. Have a pillow fight at bedtime.

957. Tell your mate that he is fun to be with. Be sure that you are someone who is fun to be around.

958. Place a heart by your name when you sign your cards and letters.

959. Stop an elevator between floors and have a mini-make-out session.

960. Squeeze into a photo booth together and capture your mugs on film.

961. Write a love story together. What can you learn from each other's storylines?

962. Stop trying to be like the Joneses in the romance department. Learn to be comfortable being yourselves.

963. Give her a gorgeous lace apron when you know that she is planning a special dinner for the two of you.

964. Make love in every room of your house or apartment (hallways, attics, and large closets count).

965. Share your "I've always wanted to" stories. It could be that your mate feels the same way.

966. Show pride in your lover's accomplishments. Be part of his team.

967. When you bring breakfast to your mate in bed, make a grand production of it. Have a tray, flowers, good dishes, and the morning paper.

968. Stop all the competition between you and your mate. Competition is a huge romance killer.

The worst prison would be a closed heart.
—Pope John Paul II

969. Learn to use friendly persuasion on your mate instead of ugly ultimatums.

970. Slip out early on your next meeting, party, or sporting event just to spend some time with your significant other.

971. Fix s'mores in the fireplace on a winter's evening and just chat about your lives, love, and dreams.

972. Plan a vacation months in advance to give yourselves something fun to look forward to together.

973. Always laugh at your love's jokes (even the bad ones). Never laugh at your lover.

974. At least once a month, do something nice for your mate, but don't let him know that you are the one who did it.

975. Place a beautiful Baccarat carafe by her bedside with a note saying that she is the water to your soul.

976. Give a practical mate a romantically practical gift, such as:
     - ✦ Securities
     - ✦ Mutual funds
     - ✦ Real estate
     - ✦ Stocks

     For the romantic part, give ones that have a romantic link to them.

977. Place little love ads in every newspaper in your city declaring your love for her. If your love gets embarrassed easily, use your pet names for each other.

978. Give him a home theater system filled with romantic movies.

979. While she is away on a business trip, make some romantic changes to your home.

980. Allow time for your love for each other to deepen and become stronger.

981. Act on your romantic impulses to create passionate memories.

982. For a little lunchtime treat, take a yummy box lunch over to your mate's office and share your lunch hours.

983. Book a Valentine's Day or Sweetest Day overnight at a grand hotel or a quaint inn. Reserve your room early, as the best rooms get booked months in advance.

984. Have your florist design a lovely heart-shaped topiary for your love's desk or mantel.

985. Know the true "friends" of romance:
     - ✦ Babysitters
     - ✦ Mad money
     - ✦ Good timing
     - ✦ Holidays
     - ✦ Trips

986. Learn the difference between being romantic and being too romantic for your own good.

987. For men only: Give up your macho demeanor.

988. Wish your lover sweet dreams at midnight.

989. Fact: Optimists have better love lives than pessimists. Be upbeat. Look on the bright side of life.

990. Make use of daily affirmations to make you more romantic and a better mate.

991. Give your mate a pretty jar of green jellybeans.

992. Put a touch of lace around your home for a more romantic feel:
    - ✦ On pantry shelves
    - ✦ On pillowcases
    - ✦ On towels
    - ✦ On placemats

993. Take up a relaxing pastime where the two of you can enjoy the activity but still visit with each other:
    - ✦ Horseback riding
    - ✦ Herb gardening
    - ✦ Fishing
    - ✦ Antiquing
    - ✦ Canoeing
    - ✦ Backpacking
    - ✦ Cooking

994. Buy a tablet of Post-it Notes and use them to write tiny love notes.

A successful marriage is an edifice that must be rebuilt every day.
—André Maurois

995. Send your lover a scrapbook filled with memorabilia from your relationship.

996. Serenade your sweetie beneath her bedroom window. Or, if you are too shy, hire a musician to play a special song for her.

997. Fill her hope chest with lovely, dreamlike gifts.

998. Always give Christmas/Hanukkah gifts to your lover.

999. Turn Valentine's Day into a huge holiday that both of you look forward to celebrating each year.

1000. Be a "middle mate." Have:
    - ✦ Middle-of-the-week dates
    - ✦ Middle-of-the-day dates
    - ✦ Middle-of-the-night dates
    - ✦ A midyear date

ROMANTIC RULE #6
True romantics know that romance happens
365 days a year and not just on Valentine's Day.

1001. Get friends to help you in the romance department:
   ✦ Chauffeuring ✦ Surprising
   ✦ Catering   ✦ Babysitting

1002. On big birthdays, use the candles that refuse to get blown out and ask your lover to keep making romantic wishes.

1003. Give the cook a break, by bringing home dinner and spending the time together instead of one of you slaving away in the kitchen.

1004. Make love in front of a roaring fire.

1005. In February, it is easy to find lots of newspaper articles on relationships, love, and gift giving. Send any appropriate articles to your lover to get him thinking about romance.

1006. Learn to surprise your mate in ways that don't cost you anything:
   ✦ An unexpected kiss or hug
   ✦ A hidden love note
   ✦ Singing to your love

1007. Whenever you travel on business, try to bring a little trinket back for your lover.

> *He who marries might be sorry.*
> *He who does not will be sorry.*
> —**Czechoslovakian proverb**

1008. Give your love a beautiful box of stationery with hearts or roses on it. Or give a lovely box engraved with her initials.

1009. Replace all the books in your den with:
   ✦ Romance novels
   ✦ Books of poetry
   ✦ Relationship self-help books

1010. Make arrangements with the airline to have a gift brought to your love with her meal. She'll be the envy of all her seatmates.

1011. Take a midnight ride in the country on a hot summer's night.

1012. Instead of just dancing one dance at a dance or reception, make it a priority to dance every dance with your love.

1013. Send her a new nightie every Friday for a month.

1014. Make scrolls out of your love letters. Write your thoughts on heavy-stock paper and then roll and tie them with pretty ribbons.

1015. Call your florist and ask what the rarest flower is that is currently in stock. Send a bouquet of these blooms with a note saying that your love for each other is rarer and more precious than the flowers.

1016. Send a beautiful invitation to your mate's office inviting her out for a fabulous, dream date.

1017. Hang a lovely gold necklace on her car mirror and wait for her to find it when she starts her car.

1018. If you were high school sweethearts, get dressed up in your old prom clothes and spend the evening dancing to your old music.

1019. Pretend that you don't even know each other and try to pick each other up.

1020. Ask your fraternity or sorority members to serenade your love.

1021. Ask your best friend to plan a mystery date for the two of you and then call your mate with an invitation to the mystery date.

1022. If you don't have time to write a long love letter, send a love note.

1023. Compose new lyrics to "your song." Sing it to your mate on a karaoke machine to get the best effect.

1024. Give her a darling CD house filled with romantic music.

The loving are the daring.
—Bayard Taylor

1025. Before you leave on a business trip, mail a "missing you" card that will arrive on the day you leave town.

1026. Some suggested occasions to give your lover a gift:
    ✦ Your mate got a promotion.
    ✦ Your mate had a really bad day.
    ✦ Your mate got fired (a really, really bad day).
    ✦ Your mate had lunch with an old flame.
    ✦ An old flame called your mate.
    ✦ Your mate's best friend got a divorce.
    ✦ Your mate's best friend got a huge promotion.

♦ There is a new store in town.

♦ There is a new florist in town.

♦ Your mate did you a big favor.

1027. When your love goes on a business trip, buy her a new cosmetic bag and fill it with travel-size soaps and lotions.

1028. Instead of picking your mate up at the airport as planned, surprise him. Show up at his hotel and arrange to stay together one more night. This idea takes some planning to pull off. Check with your lover's boss to arrange the day off, change the airline ticket departure date, and be sure that this will work with his business schedule.

1029. At an old-fashioned soda fountain, split a banana split.

1030. Make a gigantic greeting card out of an old movie poster. Pick one of your favorite love stories and then write a romantic message on the poster.

1031. Ask all her friends to write a one-line compliment about her. Frame them and give them to her when she is going through a rough time.

1032. Slip a framed picture of yourself in his suitcase the next time he is called out of town on business so that he won't forget you.

1033. Give a world-class gift such as a:

♦ Home   ♦ Show dog

♦ Car   ♦ Yacht

♦ Vacation home   ♦ Expensive piece of jewelry

1034. If you simply can't bring yourself to unplug the phone, at least use your answering machine to handle all calls that happen during romantic moments.

1035. If your mate loves to cook, give:

♦ A library of cookbooks

♦ Fine cookware

♦ Cooking lessons

♦ A note of appreciation after he fixes a special meal

1036. Pretend to be busy and then, at the last minute, surprise her with a fabulous dream date.

1037. For men only: Compliment her on her:
   - ✦ Career
   - ✦ Appearance
   - ✦ Clothing
   - ✦ Hair
   - ✦ Cooking
   - ✦ Home décor

1038. For women only: Compliment him on his:
   - ✦ Job performance
   - ✦ Appearance
   - ✦ Car
   - ✦ Athletic ability

1039. Spend an entire evening looking through your wedding photographs together.

1040. Decorate your bedroom in your mate's favorite color.

1041. Give her a new mini-wardrobe of clothing, shoes, lingerie, and a handbag in her favorite colors.

1042. Learn to play the guitar or the piano so that you can perform some romantic songs for your lover.

1043. Pass on great romance. If you have a unique way to show that you care, share the tip with your friends.

1044. Hire a masseuse to come to your home and give you and your mate a great massage.

1045. Attend a concert in the park on a Sunday afternoon and arrange beforehand to have the band dedicate a song to your lover.

1046. Do you want to be extravagant and take your mate out for a memorable date, but your budget is tight? Instead of having dinner at an expensive restaurant, have cocktails in the bar instead—and then take your lover back to your place for a fabulous home-cooked meal.

> *Have a heart that never hardens,*
> *a temper that never tires,*
> *a touch that never hurts.*
> —Charles Dickens

1047. Travel a cross-country trip and stay only at romantic hotels or inns.

1048. To be a great lover, try to live in the moment, at least during romantic ones.

1049. Plan an elegant date:
- ✦ Dinner at a five-star restaurant
- ✦ Ballet
- ✦ Opera
- ✦ Theater
- ✦ Symphony

1050. Take your dog-loving mate to the best dog show of them all—the Westminster Dog Show in New York City—and arrange to give her a puppy after the big show. It is in February each year.

The secret of a happy marriage is simple:
Just keep on being as polite to one another
as you are to your best friends.
—Robert Quillen

1051. Buy a blank book and write out a love story for her to read.

1052. Make dinner a bit more exciting tonight by hiding a love note in his napkin saying that you are the dessert course.

1053. How about a touch of sophistication for him? Give him an elegant smoking jacket along with some fine cigars.

1054. For a wonderfully fragrant gift, send a gardenia plant instead of flowers.

1055. Write a mission statement for your relationship and frame it so that you both can see it regularly.

1056. Frame prints from cities that you have visited together. Create a special wall in your home of memories from your great trips together.

1057. Have a selection of "mood" sheets:
- ✦ Flannels for cold nights
- ✦ Floral for spring and summer
- ✦ Satins for romantic times

1058. Give him a wardrobe of a new shirt and tie for each day of the week.

1059. Tell each other all about your times apart so that both of you will feel comfortable with each other's absences.

1060. Overlook each other's faults (okay, so you don't have any, but don't look at his).

1061. Give a book of gift certificates to a movie theater with instructions that the coupons can be used only for romantic or foreign films on dates with you.

1062. Pick a theme for her gifts, such as:
    + **Pamper Day:** cosmetics, lotions, and beauty treatment gift certificates
    + **Career Day:** work-related new wardrobe, briefcase, pen
    + **Pet Day:** puppy with all the trimmings
    + **Hobby Day:** accessories that tie in with her special interest
    + **Relationship Day:** romantic best-sellers along with coupons for great dates

1063. Give her a "plot" of her diamond (call a jeweler who specializes in diamonds) so that she can always know that she has the right stone.

1064. Have a bouquet delivered by a special messenger and be sure to include a very romantic note with the flowers.

1065. Send a lovely box of gourmet foods instead of candy. Make sure that it includes all of her favorites.

1066. Decorate her birthday cake with edible flowers for a touch of elegance.

1067. Place a pair of satin slippers by her old, scruffy slippers with a note saying that she is your Cinderella.

1068. Hibernate together during a major snowstorm. Turn your home into a cozy love nest for the duration of the blizzard.

1069. Get into the habit of thinking about romance and love throughout your day. You have to really work at this at first, but after a couple of weeks it will become automatic to you.

1070. Keep a postcard scrapbook of all the cards you send to each other. You will cherish it in the years ahead.

1071. Prepare a basket of pet toys for her new puppy or sick dog. Remember: The way to a dog lover's heart is through her dog.

1072. Always thank your mate for a date. Stop taking each other for granted.

1073. Give your dog-loving mate an oil painting of his four-legged buddy.

1074. After a great movie or musical production that your mate loved, send a soundtrack CD as a way to show that you care and enjoyed the show on your date.

1075. "Look" at your lover through your sense of touch.

1076. Present a height-challenged mate with a romantically decorated footstool to make it easier for her to get things out of closets and cabinets.

1077. Browse an art supply store to pick up unique gift finds such as a paint-by-number kit for two.

1078. Give your love a work of art that speaks to his soul and will remind him of you.

1079. Shop for gifts for your mate while the two of you are on vacation. Later, for holidays, give these gifts and your mate will be very impressed.

1080. Spend Saturday morning in bed together instead of running errands. The world won't fall apart and it will be good for the two of you.

1081. Give a lifetime-supply gift of:
    ✦ Candles
    ✦ Dishes with roses or hearts
    ✦ Satin sheets
    ✦ Fine wine or champagne
    ✦ Romantic art for the whole house
    ✦ Romantic music
    ✦ Romantic books

1082. For a change of pace, try giving unique, out-of-print romance novels. Search for them at specialized bookstores, book auctions, flea markets, antiques shops, and online.

1083. Bestow a twin gift on your mate. If your lover likes a certain item, purchase two of them.

1084. Before a big night out on the town, thrill her with a new cocktail dress and accessories.

1085. Paint her toenails for her. Treat her to your first ever pedicure and foot massage combo.

1086. Instead of sending a bouquet of flowers, send a single orchid. It is a lovely, understated way to say you care.

1087. Bring her flowers for her hair. Ask your florist for tea roses or violets.

1088. On a hot summer day, braid your love's long locks of hair to keep her cool.

1089. Do a little research and give her the newest item in the world of fashion. Look through the current issue of *Vogue* or *Harper's Bazaar* to get some ideas.

1090. Give up the notions that romance is:
    ✦ Too much work   ✦ For other people
    ✦ For singles only   ✦ For couples without children
    ✦ For young lovers

1091. Hide a ring inside a lovely English enamel box. Choose a box with a great romantic saying on it.

1092. When you give a present:
    ✦ Make it something your mate really wants.
    ✦ Beautifully gift-wrap it.
    ✦ Present it in an unusual way.
    ✦ Give it at an unexpected moment.

The only reward of virtue is virtue;
the only way to have a true friend is
to be a true friend.
—Ralph Waldo Emerson

1093. Strive to be young at heart again. It will help you to be more creative, and it is one of the best ways to keep romance alive.

1094. Give the gift of romantic lingerie:
    ✦ For men: silk robes, smoking jackets, pajamas
    ✦ For women: gowns, robes

1095. Send a beautiful wedding anniversary cake to her at the office to let her know that you are thinking of her on your special day.

1096. Mail a restaurant gift certificate with a notation that the two of you on your next "romance" anniversary must use it.

1097. Keep in mind that one of the best ways to be romantic is to learn the fine art of etiquette. Read Emily Post or Miss Manners to learn all about the social graces.

1098. Reasons to put romance to work in your relationship:
  + You will feel closer to your lover.
  + Your mate will feel loved.
  + Your mate will feel special.
  + It is fun.
  + Your relationship will improve.
  + It is sexy.
  + Your mate will love you for it.
  + Great lovers are always romantic!

1099. Never use romantic gestures to get you out of the "doghouse." If you need to get out of trouble, use the words "I'm sorry" or "I was wrong." Romance is to add fire to your love, not to calm a temper.

1100. Give a timeless gift of love such as:
  + A gold watch
  + An anniversary ring
  + Pearls
  + A gold heart-shaped locket
  + A cameo
  + A charm bracelet
  + An engagement ring
  + A three-stone anniversary ring
  + Monogrammed cuff links

1101. If you gave her an engagement ring years ago and can now afford a more extravagant one, propose to her all over again with a new, dazzling ring.

1102. Dance the night away:
  + At home to the radio
  + At a wedding reception
  + Under the stars on your patio
  + On a beach
  + At a nightclub
  + On a rooftop

1103. Give your lover a gift from Tiffany's. Everyone loves those tiny blue gift boxes.

1104. Volunteer to work for her charity to show how much you care about her and her interests. Sign up to work with her.

1105. Fix a French picnic that includes:
- ✦ A loaf of bread
- ✦ A good selection of cheese
- ✦ Fine wine
- ✦ Fresh flowers
- ✦ Candles

1106. Send a membership to a flower-of-the-month club so that she will have a year of lovely flowers to remind her of your love.

1107. Make up a reason to celebrate together this coming weekend. Turn it into a weekend that you will always remember!

1108. Enjoy your times apart instead of being "mopey" that you aren't together; that way you will bring even more to your times together.

1109. Give a romantic pep talk to an unromantic mate. Remember not to nag. Your goal is to inspire!

1110. Always be polite to each other. It is so simple and makes a world of difference in the quality of your relationship.

1111. Be your own version of Christopher Columbus and look for new romantic places that the two of you can explore.

1112. Plan a party where everyone brings stories or mementos of your relationship. Invite everyone you know to join in your celebration.

1113. Host a gigantic yard sale to get rid of all his ex's stuff. Use the money to buy stuff for the two of you.

1114. Together, seek out the:
- ✦ Unfamiliar
- ✦ Unknown
- ✦ Unusual

1115. When you can't sleep, make love.

1116. Rub his temples when he has a headache. Get an ice pack to soothe his head. Take good care of him.

1117. Hide fresh flowers in the washing machine to make even the most boring task a little bit romantic.

1118. Smooch during traffic jams (discreetly, of course). Snuggle. Hold hands.

1119. Give him more time and energy for romance by paying a handyman to do his chores.

1120. Set off fireworks each time you enter a new phase of your relationship, such as:
- ✦ Dating each other exclusively
- ✦ Getting engaged
- ✦ Getting married
- ✦ Big anniversaries
- ✦ Having a baby
- ✦ Getting back together after a breakup
- ✦ Making up after a huge fight
- ✦ Falling in love all over again

1121. Good lovers are good listeners, so learn the art of listening:
- ✦ Remain still and quiet while your mate talks.
- ✦ Refrain from telling your story—just let your mate talk.
- ✦ Ask questions.
- ✦ Don't interrupt.
- ✦ Lean forward.
- ✦ Keep your eyes on your mate.

1122. Be sure to pull your own romantic weight in the relationship. In other words, you can't expect your mate to be romantic if you aren't.

1123. Treat every day as if it were Thanksgiving and have a sense of gratitude about your relationship. Count your blessings. Say a prayer of thanks together.

1124. Set up a scholarship fund in your lover's name if he is academically minded.

Trust your hunches. They're usually based on facts filed away just below the conscious level.
—Dr. Joyce Brothers

1125. If your mate suffers from a health concern, donate medical equipment to a hospital in her name.

1126. Let your guard down when you are together. Let him see the real you. Let him know of your true feelings for him.

1127. Romantic environments are:
      - Smoke-free
      - Pollution-free
      - Stress-free
      - Clutter-free
      - Quiet and peaceful

1128. Celebrate birthdays and anniversaries with an attitude of fun, excitement, and extravagance.

1129. Stop your tit-for-tat thinking. It will only cause you more heartache.

1130. Spend the next twenty-four hours together away from your children. Call your parents and ask them to baby-sit for your spur-of-the-moment romantic retreat.

1131. Perform a selfless act for your mate just because you are a nice guy.

1132. Qualities of a topnotch lover:
      - Spontaneous
      - Open
      - Honest
      - Spiritual
      - Vital
      - Kind
      - Self-sufficient
      - Loving
      - Joyful
      - Gentle

1133. Take your lover to Cumberland Falls State Park resort in Kentucky to view the romantic, natural wonder of rainbows by moonlight.

1134. Give a writing pen that has hearts all over it for your mate to use when addressing your wedding invitations.

1135. Encourage your mate's hobbies by giving little gifts:
      - **Tennis:** apparel, balls, new racket
      - **Jogging:** shoes, clothes, case of sports drinks
      - **Bowling:** bag, ball, glove, gift certificates for lane time
      - **Painting:** art supplies, lessons, smock
      - **Dogs:** books on a particular breed, obedience class gift certificate, toys, leash, treats
      - **Reading:** books, bookmarks, new reading glasses
      - **Cooking:** cookbooks, kitchen gadgets, cooking lessons, great cookware

1136. Give a subscription to a magazine that pertains to your mate's interests. Browse a bookstore to find all kinds of unique magazines.

1137. Present her with a pretty Madame Alexander doll that relates to her favorite romantic heroine, such as:

    ✦ Cinderella   ✦ Scarlet O'Hara   ✦ Juliet

1138. Hide a lovely set of Limoges dessert plates in the dishwasher for her to find with a note saying that you loved dinner last night.

1139. Fill her desk with snacks for when she is too busy to meet you for lunch. We recommend little sweetheart cakes along with her standard favorite goodies.

1140. Make her feel loved by checking on her when she is home alone on a dark and stormy night.

1141. If she didn't receive her ideal wedding gifts when the two of you got married, why not buy some of them for an unexpected "postwedding party for two." We suggest:

    ✦ Fine china   ✦ Lovely table linens
    ✦ Sterling flatware   ✦ Beautiful serving pieces
    ✦ Crystal goblets

1142. Even if you stay at home on New Year's Eve, make it a party for two and a big deal, by:

    ✦ Dressing up   ✦ Throwing confetti
    ✦ Playing lively music   ✦ Sipping champagne
    ✦ Wearing party hats   ✦ Kissing at midnight
    ✦ Blowing horns at midnight ✦ Setting off fireworks

1143. On Groundhog Day, if he sees his shadow, hibernate together for the rest of the winter.

1144. Dress in your green jammies and stay home to celebrate St. Patrick's Day.

1145. If your sweetheart is a mom, for Mother's Day send a gift that lets her know that you still think of her as a lover and not just the mother of your children. Also, make sure that the children all remember her with nice gifts.

1146. Replace the practical items in your home with elegant versions of them, such as:
- ✦ Paper bookmarks: sterling markers
- ✦ Plastic letter opener: sterling opener
- ✦ Bic pen: Montblanc writing instrument
- ✦ Cookie jar: crystal biscuit box

1147. On Thanksgiving morning, present her with a list of reasons why you are most grateful to have her in your life. Pray a prayer of gratitude for your relationship together.

1148. Make it a "picnic day" by preparing a picnic for each meal and enjoying the feasts in three romantic locations. Put some thought and effort into the day. Pack some yummy meals and bring along some candles and soft music. Don't forget to bring along a pretty picnic blanket and some bug spray.

The best way you can surprise a woman with an anniversary gift is to give her just what she wanted.
—Arbuth Arundale

1149. Savor the last night of summer by sharing a meal served outdoors under the stars.

1150. Surprise her with a private lingerie shower, but with a twist. Give her items that she would love to have on a cold winter night:
- ✦ Flannel PJs
- ✦ Chenille bathrobe
- ✦ Bunny slippers
- ✦ Wool sleep socks

Just be sure that all the items have a heart motif of some kind.

1151. If your love wears a uniform to work, buy her a new one of a different style and attach a note that says, "Our love never goes out of style."

1152. Remember the moment that you fell in love with your mate and write a love letter telling your love all about it. Turn it into a long epic story. We promise that she won't be able to put it down.

1153. Just for one date, speak with a French accent because it sounds romantic and sexy. Whisper sweet nothings. Be playful and silly.

1154. Be a sneak! When you are shopping at an outdoor fair or market, make a mental note of what your mate admires and split up and buy it. After the two of you get home, give it to your love for a welcome surprise.

1155. If your mate drives a lot, fill his car with items such as:

- ✦ Maps
- ✦ A blanket
- ✦ A flashlight
- ✦ Flares
- ✦ Snacks
- ✦ A compass
- ✦ Love notes
- ✦ A map back to your home

1156. Send her a half-dozen birds of paradise in a lovely tall vase.

1157. Use your connections to help your mate's career or social standing. Network for him.

1158. Find out which title your mate prefers:

- ✦ Significant other
- ✦ Partner
- ✦ Wife/husband
- ✦ Better half
- ✦ Lover
- ✦ Boyfriend/girlfriend

Maybe he prefers his own title, so ask him!

1159. Tie bows with red ribbons around all the trees in your backyard and attach a love note to each before you host a patio dinner for two.

1160. Give her lots of heart-shaped pillows. Decorate your home with them.

1161. Start collecting lovely candlesticks, as romantics can never have too many.

1162. Give a gift of the other precious metal—platinum. Add a diamond to it to make it a spectacular gift.

1163. Share a yummy dessert. Don't count calories. Treat yourselves and be a little decadent!

1164. When you dine at an elegant restaurant, feed him a taste of your dinner even though you want to savor each bite.

1165. Ways to tell if you are a true romantic:

- ✦ You celebrate unusual anniversaries.
- ✦ You call for no real reason.

- ✦ You look forward to Valentine's Day.
- ✦ You have lingerie instead of PJs.
- ✦ You have lots of candles in your home.
- ✦ You write love letters.
- ✦ You have sent a greeting card in the last few weeks.
- ✦ You plan dates.
- ✦ You have lots of romantic CDs.
- ✦ You own plenty of romantic movies.
- ✦ You read about relationship issues.
- ✦ You put lots of effort into your love life.
- ✦ Your mate thinks you are great.

1166. Romantics know that all couples have periods of closeness and then periods of moving away from each other. It is like a couple's dance, and the trick is to hang in there during the moving-away periods.

1167. If you love her name (and you had better, or you will be in deep trouble), monogram all kinds of gifts for her:
    - ✦ Towels
    - ✦ Stationery
    - ✦ Tote bags
    - ✦ Shirts
    - ✦ T-shirts

1168. In love and life, it is perseverance that makes a huge difference. Hang in there during the rough spots.

1169. Sometimes, less is more. Give one fabulous gift instead of several small gifts.

1170. Spray a touch of cologne in his car before he leaves on a road trip as a subtle reminder of your relationship.

1171. Straighten your lover's closet and add some new garments. Buy her that special outfit that she has been dying to have.

1172. For a mate who is a shoe lover, give a wardrobe of new shoes.

1173. Change:
    - ✦ Your routines
    - ✦ Your usual holiday plans
    - ✦ Your dating habits
    - ✦ Your normal vacation plans

    Change breaks the old boring patterns that ruin romance.

1174. Dance together to the latest hit CD of romantic music.

1175. When you won't be spending the night together, give her a beautiful bed jacket to keep her warm. Or hide a teddy under the covers for her to find.

1176. Encourage your love to go after her dreams. Help her achieve them.

1177. Three nice words that will make a big change in her attitude for the evening: "I'll cook dinner."

1178. Rent the offbeat but wonderful love story *Regarding Henry*.

1179. Go to a confectionery and ask them to make a special treat for your love. Or have them create a box made up of all of his or her favorites.

1180. Fix a vending machine out of an old, large box for your lover that gives coupons instead of treats. Write your own coupons, such as these:
  ✦ Good for a kiss
  ✦ Valid for a batch of homemade cookies
  ✦ Good for a hug
  ✦ Valid for a back rub
  ✦ Good for the date of your choice

1181. Draw hearts on your envelopes. Turn a plain envelope into a masterpiece.

1182. Order a set of bar glasses with both of your initials on them. Use them to serve your morning juice.

1183. Give your car-loving mate some new hubcaps and enclose a note saying that his love makes your world go around.

1184. Create a heart-shaped goldfish pond for your garden. Hire a landscape designer to help you if you feel that this is a bit more than you can tackle on your own.

1185. Head to a fun culinary shop to buy every utensil, gadget, and pan that is heart-shaped.

1186. Make your bed together. Who knows where that will lead!

1187. Buy matching:

- ✦ Jogging suits
- ✦ PJs
- ✦ Robes
- ✦ Ski outfits
- ✦ T-shirts
- ✦ Christmas sweaters
- ✦ Mufflers
- ✦ Team jerseys

1188. Add red food coloring to the water and use an ice tray with heart shapes to make some romantic ice cubes.

1189. Don't set a romantic table for two. Instead set a beautiful table for one and then wait on your lover at dinner.

1190. Give a box of delicious chocolate-covered cherries or strawberries. So yummy!

1191. Make a batch of Rice Krispies Treats in the shape of teddy bears and put red icing hearts on them. Serve to your mate.

1192. Give a second chance to your first marriage (while you are still married)! Get professional help if you need it.

1193. Hold hands in public. Come on, be romantic. You can do it!

1194. Plan on growing old together. Talk about it. Make plans.

1195. Never compare one relationship to another. All relationships are unique.

1196. Place a mistletoe wreath on your bedroom door.

1197. Read this book together and highlight ideas that you both love. Make plans to try them.

1198. Know that romance should be an acknowledgment of love, not confused with love.

1199. Take a romantic hot-air balloon ride together. Plan to go out to eat afterwards at a quaint restaurant to celebrate your flight.

1200. Remember to build bridges and not walls.

ROMANTIC RULE #7
Tailor your romantic gestures to suit your mate's idea of romance.

1201. Give your lover a flawless diamond to represent your flawless love affair.

1202. Keep in mind that the act of caring is love in motion. Have a heart-to-heart talk about what each of you really needs to feel loved and special.

1203. Know that being in love should be an active rather than a passive pursuit.

1204. Ask her to dance even when the dance floor is empty. Don't be shy.

1205. Call her the Queen of Hearts. Call him the King of Diamonds.

1206. Develop a strong sense of "we-ness" instead of "me-ness." Think about what is best for the two of you as a couple.

1207. Make her royalty, at least for a day. Take her to the palace at Monte Carlo.

1208. When you hit rock bottom in your relationship, take a break from each other. Each of you give the other some space. You will appreciate each other a lot more when you get back together.

1209. Accept the fact that you must understand a person before you can truly love him or her. True love takes time.

1210. For men only: Know that married men live longer and have better health than single or divorced men.

1211. To save you and your lover from relationship disasters, admit when you are wrong. Admit to yourself when you are wrong and then to your partner.

1212. Have a relationship checkup once a month to talk about:
   ✦ Any problems
   ✦ Your feelings
   ✦ What direction you want the relationship to take
   ✦ Plans that involve the two of you

The best relationship is the one in which your love for each other exceeds your need for each other.
—Author Unknown

1213. Celebrate the first day of spring each March by sending her a beautiful bouquet of spring flowers.

1214. Stop what you are doing whenever the two of you are alone and hear "your song" being played, and dance.

1215. Give three compliments to make up for every piece of criticism that you give your mate. Try not to give many criticisms.

1216. Send her a telegram when she is in the hospital and you are away on a business trip.

1217. Take him out for lunch along with some of his best buddies. Dress up. Spoil them. Let his friends see just how wonderful you are.

1218. Have a magician perform a new version of the "disappearing ring act." This time, though, have him produce an engagement ring for your lover.

1219. Hire a dance instructor to coach you both privately before your next big social gathering. Have fun learning to dance together. Practice by candlelight or moonlight.

1220. Get a satellite system just because you want to watch more romantic movies.

1221. Ask a talented gardener to cut your shrubbery into heart shapes. (Try this in your backyard.)

1222. Throw an "unbirthday" party or an "it's not our anniversary" party for your lover.

1223. Ask him to a Sadie Hawkins dance for two. Or throw a big turn-around dance party with your girlfriends and ask all of the great men in your lives.

1224. Once every year, give a major gift for no special reason other than romance. Be sure to do it when she won't suspect that it is coming her way.

1225. Call ticket agencies to obtain lists of upcoming events that your lover would enjoy. Purchase great tickets for some upcoming events for the two of you—give yourselves fun plans to look forward to in the future.

1226. Arrange for both of you to get a leave of absence from work so that you can go on an extended vacation together.

1227. Turn Saturday nights into special events. After all, there are only fifty-two in an entire year, so you can't afford to squander them being couch potatoes.

1228. Everyone believes that romance is important before you get married, but we are telling you that it is even more important after you marry.

1229. Put Caller ID on your phone line so that you will always know when he calls. When he phones, be sure to answer using a warm and friendly tone of voice.

1230. After you are married, take your mate out on the anniversary of your rehearsal dinner. Talk about the old days.

1231. Little ways to celebrate Valentine's Day:
   ✦ Wear red.
   ✦ Send zillions of children's Valentines to your love.
   ✦ Give all types of Valentine candy.
   ✦ Give homemade cards.
   ✦ Give homemade goodies.
   ✦ Meet for a coffee break.
   ✦ Call to just say hello and Happy Valentine's Day.
   ✦ Dine by candlelight.
   ✦ Play romantic music.
   ✦ Plan a fun date together.

1232. Bake him an angel food cake when he is being heavenly to you.

1233. Our "rules" for great relationships:
   ✦ Be honest.   ✦ Laugh often.
   ✦ Fight fair.   ✦ Pray.
   ✦ Love unconditionally.   ✦ Stay committed.

1234. Take your love out to dinner to celebrate the good things that happen in his life.

1235. Install a hot tub in your home. Use it to unwind together.

1236. Many people have replaced letter writing with e-mail or faxes, but there is nothing more romantic than receiving a handwritten love letter.

1237. Tie dozens of balloons to your fence with a Welcome Home sign.

1238. When she needs a lift, give her a piggyback ride.

1239. Take your love to a trendy bistro to celebrate an offbeat anniversary.

1240. Surprise him by showing up in a disguise when he is working late and dining alone at the office.

1241. Sleep in a:
     + Four-poster bed
     + Brass bed
     + Bunk bed
     + Twin bed (together)
     + Canopy bed
     + Hammock

1242. Turn her dreams into a real-life wedding by getting married at Cinderella's castle at Disney World. Check with your travel agent for details. Or go online at *www.disneyworld.com*.

1243. Together, hold an unusual bonfire: Burn all your Rolodex cards with names of former lovers. Burn your old black book of old flames.

1244. Arrange to attend a prom together at your old high school. Okay, you may have to just go as chaperones this time, but take advantage of the fun atmosphere.

1245. Stop complaining to your friends about the relationship. If you don't like something, take positive steps to change it instead of just whining about it.

1246. Have zillions of candles burning when she gets home from the office.

1247. Learn the art of empathy. In other words, imagine being in your mate's shoes.

1248. Fill a kitchen canister with heart-shaped candy and flowers.

1249. Give her a painting of the church where you were married. Be sure to have it beautifully framed.

1250. Expect the romantic best from your mate. In time, you'll get it!

1251. Hide a piece of chocolate inside her jewelry box beside her engagement ring.

1252. Buy a set of index cards and a pretty file box to keep them in. Write a love note on every one of the cards. Present it to your mate after your next date for a wonderful surprise.

1253. Rub scented lotion on her chapped winter hands.

A happy marriage is a long conversation that always seems too short.
—André Maurois

1254. Bring along a few of your favorite framed photographs of the two of you for your hotel room when you travel. It will bring back some happy memories and make your room seem more intimate.

1255. For more privacy, travel during the off-seasons. Dine out on Monday nights.

1256. Give her a romantic fantasy knickknack. How about a Cinderella coach teapot or cookie jar?

1257. Get a huge box, punch some air holes in it, get inside, have a friend gift-wrap it (leaving the air holes uncovered), and have it delivered to your mate.

1258. Plan to have a memory night when the two of you must bring five happy shared memories on note cards to share.

1259. Send a cookie bouquet instead of flowers.

1260. Serve oysters and champagne and see what happens!

1261. Spend a night in a castle or mansion. Remember that atmosphere is important to romance. Ask your travel agent for some suggestions.

1262. Create a romantic bubble bath by buying red or pink tinted soap.

1263. Create a mini–herb garden for your gourmet cook on her kitchen window ledge.

1264. Make her feel like a topnotch model. Send her to a glamorous photography studio and have them work their magic.

1265. Surprise her with a diamond solitaire whose carat weight matches the number of years that you have been together or the number of decades that you have been together.

1266. Be a good sport and take her to her family reunion and turn it into a romantic mini-vacation. Plan some fun dates away from the reunion.

1267. Read the story of Romeo and Juliet to each other.

1268. On a special evening, dress in romantic vintage clothing.

1269. Pick out wedding gifts for friends together. Always get into that romantic frame of mind, any way that you can.

1270. Dance the "Anniversary Waltz" only with your lover.

If you were arrested for kindness, would there be enough evidence to convict you?
—Author Unknown

1271. Open a Visa or MasterCard account for your love with a huge credit balance before her next shopping expedition.

1272. Always help each other get through life's ups and downs, but try to add as many romantic touches as you can.

1273. If your mate is trying to stop smoking and is using patches, cut them into little heart shapes.

1274. Check out the latest books on birth order to learn how it can affect a couple's relationship.

1275. Treat your love to a new, beautiful smile: Give your love braces. Or give a gift certificate to have her teeth whitened.

1276. Tell her she is smart.

1277. Tell her she is sexy.

1278. Give her a classic gift, but with a twist—pearls with a difference:
   ✦ Black pearls   ✦ Seed pearls   ✦ Freshwater pearls

Ask your jeweler to show you a selection.

1279. Treat her to a kissing wardrobe—a new tube of lipstick for each day of the week.

1280. Don't consider breaking up as a passport to freedom. Think of it as a huge mistake.

1281. Make love from sunset to sunrise.

1282. Make love from sunrise to sunset.

1283. Studies confirm that couples who are in good physical condition enjoy sex more than those who aren't in good shape. Get in shape.

1284. Have a steady circle of close "couple" friends. Create a group of friends who will really support your relationship.

1285. Consult your mate before making plans to go out alone with your own circle of friends.

1286. Never insist on being socially active, as a couple, with someone your partner doesn't like.

1287. Keep in mind that a passionate kiss burns over twenty calories. What a great way to lose weight!

1288. After a party, enjoy your couple time of sharing "party thoughts."

1289. Pursue activities that will enable you to meet other couples who share similar interests. Sign up for lessons or join a club together.

1290. Create your own private signal to alert your love when you are ready to leave a party.

1291. Know that a fabulous sex life requires lots of emotional foreplay.

1292. Sex is not about performance, so get that silly notion out of your head.

1293. Secrets of staying in love:
  + Flexibility   + Forgiveness
  + Fun   + Commitment

1294. Long-term lovers agree: lovemaking improves with time.

1295. Give feedback to your lover on ways to improve your sex life. Be honest, but use tact.

1296. Do a remake of the society page of your Sunday newspapers: Cut out a couple of photos and replace them with photos of the two of you. Add some fun captions, and wait for your mate's reaction as he or she skims through the paper.

1297. Camp out in a sleeping bag made for two on a beautiful, star-filled night.

1298. Tuck romantic bookmarks into the books your love is currently reading.

1299. During the Christmas holidays, turn off all the lights in the house except for the Christmas tree and dream together by the glow of the tree.

1300. Create a "couple's binge day" when you eat too many chocolates, send too many flowers, and love each other even more than usual.

*It is better to understand a little
than to misunderstand a lot.*
—Anatole France

1301. Help each other maintain a strong sense of values. Stand up together for your religious beliefs.

1302. Give a gift to your lover on St. Patrick's Day for a nice little surprise. After all, most people don't give a present on this holiday, so your gift will be doubly appreciated. We suggest:
    ◆ Irish love poems
    ◆ A green after-dinner drink, crème de menthe
    ◆ Green nighties
    ◆ Green silk boxers
    ◆ Green silk tie or scarf
    ◆ Shamrock chocolates
    ◆ St. Patrick's Day T-shirt

If you cannot be a poet, be the poem.
—David Carradine

1303. Be nice to strangers just because you are in love and feeling wonderful. Besides, your kindness will come back to you both and make your relationship even better.

1304. Give her a Waterford ring holder for her engagement ring when it isn't on her finger.

1305. Thank your lover, and praise your lover, when she does romantic gestures for you. Let her know that you like having her be romantic with you.

1306. Talk. Communicate. Converse with each other regularly. Questions to open up romantic dialogues:
    ✦ What is your favorite romantic date?
    ✦ What is your most romantic memory?
    ✦ When did you fall in love?
    ✦ What gestures touch your heart the most deeply?
    ✦ When do you like to make love?
    ✦ How can we improve our love life?
    ✦ What is the most romantic thing that you can think of?
    ✦ Who is your romantic role model?
    ✦ Where is the most romantic place on Earth?

1307. Keep in mind that the more romantic gestures you make, the easier it will be for you to become a truly romantic person.

1308. It is especially important for husbands whose wives are pregnant to do extra-romantic gestures for her to keep the romance alive.

1309. Even on tiny anniversaries, use anniversary theme napkins for cocktails and also at dinner.

1310. Take a mini-mini-vacation. Take the afternoon off and go to a nearby town and have a grand time together. Do something that you two haven't done before.

1311. If you are going through a hard time in your relationship, do what the experts recommend. Fake it till you make it!

1312. Present her with a beautiful English tea set like those available from Cash's of Ireland.

1313. Spell out a message in flowers on the living room floor for your mate to find when she gets home from work.

1314. Most people spend a minimum of twelve years in school learning skills to enable themselves to get a job. Yet, most people don't spend any time learning about relationships. You need to learn how to create a healthy, loving relationship. So study romance!

1315. On cold nights, warm your hands under hot running water before you touch your lover.

1316. Sit down to meals together instead of rushing through them on your way to other activities. Linger over dessert. Catch up on your lives.

1317. Purchase a wonderful picnic basket and blanket. Make plans to put them to use for at least six romantic picnics a year.

1318. Take her on a dream fashion vacation. She doesn't pack any clothes, but buys all new ones once you get to your destination.

1319. For your walking and singing in the rain, have matching raincoats and umbrellas.

1320. Plan a romantic, good-natured prank to pull on your mate on April Fool's Day.

1321. Run your fingers through your lover's hair. Or get a Tingler and give a fantastic head massage.

1322. Buy a hammock for two for lazy summer afternoons together or for late-night stargazing.

1323. Go materialistic and give her all the tangible desires of her heart.

1324. Host a cookout for two. He can do the grilling, and you can fix the potatoes and salads. Fix dessert together.

1325. Have some memo pads printed with both of your initials or a loving sentiment.

1326. Make a giant heart out of freshly fallen snow in her front yard. Color it red with food coloring and attach a little love note. Paint a loving massage in the snow.

1327. Give your love a three-dimensional puzzle of a cupid or heart.

1328. Browse a farmer's market for fresh and different little gifts for your lover. Or stroll through the market arm-in-arm and buy things to make a great meal together.

1329. Purchase a set of matching luggage to announce to the traveling world that you are a couple.

1330. Place a dough heart on your pumpkin pie for Thanksgiving dinner. After all, isn't your mate one of your greatest blessings?

1331. Because she is so special to you, give her an angel gift:
     ✦ An ornament   ✦ A figurine   ✦ A book on angels

1332. Start a romantic book club where you and your love can lead the discussions.

1333. Spread a lovely quilt on the ground and spend the evening stargazing.

1334. Hang a heart or cupid flag outside on your anniversaries. Let the world know that the two of you are still celebrating your relationship.

1335. Attend a theater production of *Romeo and Juliet*.

1336. Kiss her hand when you part company.

> *You will find as you look back upon your life that the moments when you have truly lived are the moments when you have done things in the spirit of love.*
> —Henry Drummond

1337. Check out your local radio stations to find one that plays only love songs at night.

1338. When she is in the hospital, send her a balloon bouquet on each day she is there.

1339. Create a weeklong anniversary celebration by sending a rose to your mate. The next day, send two and so on until you reach the big day. On your anniversary send a huge rose arrangement.

1340. When you are dining out, let her order first.

1341. Place heart-shaped confetti in her briefcase when she is working really long hours, to remind her of your love.

1342. Hire a limousine to take the two of you to all your favorite spots that hold special meaning in your relationship.

1343. Use red dishes to create some very romantic table settings. Place red candles and red roses for the centerpiece.

1344. When your love is a little short of cash, present him with a bouquet or wreath made out of money.

1345. Read between the lines. It makes for some very interesting, romantic moments!

1346. Create some gift excitement on a special day by giving your most expensive gift as the last present. Let each gift that you present be more valuable than the previous one.

1347. Have a romantic bumper sticker made for his car at a print shop.

1348. When he takes an extended business trip, pack a pen, stationery, and stamps in his suitcase so that he can easily keep in touch with you.

1349. Get an audiotape of Leo Buscaglia or John Gray reading their books, to learn about love.

1350. Give her an outfit like one her favorite model wears when she goes out on the town.

1351. Hang matching Christmas stockings on the mantel for Santa to fill with romantic gifts.

1352. Get two kittens and name them after a famous couple.

1353. Visit the whimsical Mary Engelbreit store in St. Louis. She will find tons of wonderful cards and gifts that speak to her heart.

1354. When your lover gives you a compliment, accept it graciously.

1355. Wear your mate's favorite fragrance on special dates.

1356. Make friends with your lover's:
    + Family   + Friends   + Pets

1357. Keep in mind that learning to love well is a never-ending lesson in life.

1358. The only romantic gift that you can't give is trust. It must be earned!

1359. Always cuddle after sex. Forget just falling off to sleep. Great lovers stay awake.

1360. Become a one-person support group for your mate during hard times.

1361. Romantic rule: Courtship should not cease when you say "I do."

1362. Stop thinking of your lover as a home improvement project. Accept him as he is.

1363. Realize that if you put your relationship on autopilot, it will probably go off course.

1364. We hope you know that the more often you mention breaking up as a solution to your problems, the more likely it is to occur.

1365. Modern anniversary gifts:
    + **First:** clocks
    + **Fifth:** silverware
    + **Tenth:** diamond jewelry
    + **Fifteenth:** watches
    + **Twentieth:** platinum
    + **Twenty-fifth:** silver
    + **Fiftieth:** gold

1366. Stop correcting your mate's irrelevant mistakes. Ease up! You aren't his boss.

1367. Ways that romance has changed through the years:
    + Women are more assertive than ever before.
    + Dating is more relaxed.
    + Monogamy is back in style.
    + Couples are more interested in romance.
    + People are waiting longer to marry.
    + Women often pay for the dates.
    + Being a great romantic is back in style.

1368. When you spend the night at a friend's home and you are given a room with twin beds, push them together for a night of cuddling.

1369. Get matching silk pajamas or share a set of his. She gets the top and he gets the bottoms.

This above all: to thine own self be true,
and it must follow, as the night the day,
thou canst not then be false to any man.
—William Shakespeare

1370. Give her complete control of the electric blanket. You know, it is the little things that mean a lot. Or buy one with dual controls.

1371. Fold the dinner napkins into heart shapes for your next romantic dinner for two.

1372. Give him a fabulous humidor to keep his cigars nice and fresh. To make it a romantic present, fill it with chocolate cigars and rose petals when it is first given to your love.

1373. Reasons to consider marriage:
    ✦ You are in love.
    ✦ You know that your love is the one.
    ✦ You want to have a family together and you love each other.
    ✦ You know that you are ready for **this** commitment with **this** person.

1374. While you are on vacation, hang a new robe and gown in the bathroom for her to find when she steps out of the shower.

1375. Appreciate having someone to come home to in the evenings. Remember, a lot of people don't have someone special in their lives.

Look at everything as though you were seeing it
either for the first time or the last time. Then
your time on earth will be filled with glory.
—Betty Smith

1376. When you send mail to your lover, address it to his nickname instead of his formal name. Decorate the envelope.

1377. When you pray together, thank God for your relationship.

1378. Prepare a compliment jar. Take strips of paper and write sincere compliments on each one. Place all the papers in a pretty glass jar and give it to your love during a hard time in his life.

1379. Eliminate all unnecessary criticisms about your mate. Trust us, most are not necessary and they certainly are romance killers.

1380. Keep in mind that a lack of effort and commitment in your relationship is a decision to be unhappy.

1381. Traditional anniversary gifts:
     + **First:** paper   + **Twentieth:** china
     + **Fifth:** wood   + **Twenty-fifth:** silver
     + **Tenth:** tin   + **Fortieth:** ruby
     + **Fifteenth:** crystal   + **Fiftieth:** gold

1382. Cut household items into heart shapes. Use simple things such as sponges, napkins, and paper plates.

1383. When his camera has film in it, secretly take a picture of yourself holding a sign that expresses your love for him.

1384. Ask your postman for the newest stamps that look romantic. Use them on all of your mail to your mate.

1385. Hide a zillion pencils and pens in her office desk that are covered in hearts and other romantic motifs.

1386. Order some romantic personalized rubber stamps to use for love letters or on white paper as gift-wrap decorations.

1387. For a mate who loves to spend time in his or her garden, give a set of garden steps or stepping-stones that have romantic sayings on them.

1388. Give a fun little leather-and-lace gift, such as:
     + Lace gloves and a leather handbag
     + Lace socks and leather shoes

1389. While she is on an extended business trip, move her to her dream home and give her the thrill of a lifetime.

1390. For one month, give up placing demands on each other. If it improves things between you—and it will—vow to keep it up.

1391. Overwhelm her by giving a gift certificate from every:
     + Lingerie shop in town
     + Jewelry store in town

♦ Shoe store in town
♦ Candy store in town
♦ French restaurant in town

If you live in a large city, give gift certificates from shops in a certain area of your city.

1392. Place an elegant chaise longue in her bedroom to add a touch of glamour.

1393. Install a ceiling fan in your bedroom for those hot summer nights.

1394. Give your lover an interest-free loan (but ask for the interest back in hugs and kisses).

1395. Decorate his office for him in a rich style. Hire a decorator. Turn it into a room that he will love to work in. Be sure to place your photo on his desk.

1396. Give him a "manly" new vehicle such as a:

♦ Truck	♦ Jeep
♦ Moped	♦ Motorcycle
♦ Snowmobile	

ROMANTIC RULE #8
Great romantics make the most of the present moment and spontaneity is a huge part of their romantic makeup.

1397. For your anniversary, rent a classic car from the year that you met or were married.

1398. Work some overtime to make extra money to be able to afford a dream trip for the two of you.

1399. Google your mate's interest and see where it leads you. Who knows what great gift ideas you might come up with to surprise your sweetie?

1400. Place Valentine decorations throughout your home a week before the big day. Set the stage for a great holiday.

1401. Put red or pink Christmas lights on plants and trees to decorate for Valentine's Day.

1402. Bake heart-shaped cookies and cakes throughout the year.

1403. Cover up your clocks and put away your watches and just live in the moment with each other for the next twenty-four hours. Stop your normal routines and just live the way you really feel like living. Stop all of your clock-watching behaviors!

1404. Leave a trail of rose petals for her to find you.

1405. Win a prize for her at a local carnival or amusement park.

1406. When she gets a promotion, buy her a new desk set for her fabulous new office. Or give her a lovely briefcase.

1407. When your significant other moves to a new apartment, give a romantic housewarming gift such as a:
  ✦ Bottle of fine wine
  ✦ Bottle of champagne
  ✦ Painting of a beautiful garden scene
  ✦ Framed photograph of the two of you
  ✦ Heart-shaped rug
  ✦ Heart-shaped pillow

Whether it's praise, love, criticism, money, time, power, punishment, space, sorrow, laughter, need, pain, or pleasure... the more of it you give, the more of it you will receive.
—Mike Dooley

1408. Send a Waterford perfume bottle to her at the office so that she'll be the center of attention as she tells everyone just how terrific you are.

1409. Throw a romance party. Invite your friends and serve wine and heart-shaped appetizers. Ask everyone to bring an exchange gift that has a romantic theme. Be creative.

1410. Hold her gently in your arms and rock her to sleep.

1411. Stay awake all night together.

1412. Make a dream come true for your love by:
    ✦ Giving her tickets to a sold-out show
    ✦ Introducing him to a sports hero
    ✦ Proposing marriage

1413. When he wants to wear a team shirt, present him with the whole ball of wax:
    ✦ Team jacket   ✦ Team jersey
    ✦ Team sweatshirt   ✦ Team baseball cap

1414. Take a trip outside the continental United States for a touch of glamour and romance.

1415. Take a long trip aboard a fabulous ocean liner.

1416. Celebrate at least one holiday a month together. Check your calendar to see what holiday you can plan a fun event around.

1417. Write a check to your mate for a million:
    ✦ Kisses   ✦ Back rubs   ✦ Dates
    ✦ Hugs   ✦ Love letters

1418. Make a surprise deposit in her checking account before she goes shopping with her friends. Be sure to tell her about it before she heads out the door.

1419. Show you care by being extra nice to her:
    ✦ Friends   ✦ Boss   ✦ Pets
    ✦ Family   ✦ Coworkers

1420. Throw a party for her and all her closest friends at a nearby spa and pamper the entire group.

A kiss that speaks volumes
is seldom a first edition.
—Ohio State Sun Dial

1421. Get postcards of all the places you want to visit together and start sending them to him or her. To obtain the cards, contact:
    ✦ Tourism bureaus
    ✦ Museum gift shops
    ✦ Travel agents

1422. Share an intimate secret with only your mate and not your girlfriends.

1423. Play together:
    + Frolic in the swimming pool.
    + Jog hand-in-hand.
    + Dig out your old board games.
    + Visit an arcade.
    + Go to an amusement park.

    Have fun together.

1424. Close the curtains, turn off the lights, and have breakfast or lunch by candlelight.

1425. Call her your lover, as it sounds so romantic.

1426. Always be on time. That way you show respect for each other and you get to spend more time together.

1427. Too tired to cook a romantic dinner? Pick up some junk food on your way home and spend the evening just relaxing together in front of the fireplace.

1428. Create some gift excitement by giving little hints about your gift for your mate.

1429. Give up television viewing for a month and spend that time together doing fun activities instead of being couch potatoes. If you are a TV addict, agree to at least limit your TV viewing.

1430. When you are extremely busy with work, meet for breakfast or lunch instead of a dinner date. It beats not getting together at all.

1431. Start an add-a-bead, add-a-pearl, add-a-diamond, or charm bracelet for her. That way she will know that you are planning future romantic gifts.

1432. Give him a gift certificate for lawn care service to free up his weekends so that he can spend more time with you.

1433. Treat your mate better than you treat your closest friends or beloved pet.

1434. Visit a trophy shop and create a trophy for your mate. Consider:
    + World's best kisser
    + Number one mate
    + First place for great date
    + Happiest time of my life
    + World's best spouse
    + Most loved spouse
    + World's most romantic mate

1435. When you give a present, think long and hard about what your mate would like to have. Consider his tastes, not just your preferences. This tip is especially important if you and your mate do not have the same tastes.

1436. Give a beautiful music box for an anniversary gift. How about one that plays "your song" or the "Anniversary Waltz"?

1437. When shopping for a spectacular gift, you might well be on the way to making a fabulous selection if the gift seems too:
    + Expensive   + Extravagant
    + Impractical   + Outrageous

1438. Tape a flower to her bathroom mirror or hide a small bouquet underneath her bath towel.

1439. Spend a Saturday afternoon at a create-your-own-pottery store and make a romantic gift for your significant other. Paint hearts or a loving sentiment on a plate, picture frame, or statue.

1440. Spend a few minutes each day:
    + Showing your romantic feelings
    + Expressing your feelings
    + Planning upcoming dates
    + Planning celebrations
    + Thinking romantic thoughts
    + Looking on the bright side of your relationship
    + Praying for your relationship
    + Praying together
    + Spending some quality time together

Paradise is always where love dwells.
—Jean Paul F. Richter

1441. Look at your mate through rose-colored glasses. Trust us, your mate will look much better this way!

1442. Law of relationships: Little kindnesses and remembrances greatly improve the quality of one's love life. The more gestures you make, the more romance you will have!

1443. Wear a T-shirt that expresses your love for your mate. There are shops in most malls that will print up great slogans for you.

1444. If you have a habit of forgetting dates, anniversaries, and the like, get a calendar just to take care of relationship information.

1445. Tell her that you thought about her while you were at work. Let her know that she is very important in your life.

1446. Every time you travel on an extended business trip, bring back a lovely gift for your mate that shows you put time, thought, and effort into buying it.

1447. Start collecting wedding vows that you like and use them to create your own unique ceremony. Talk about them often with your significant other to learn about his or her feelings and views on love and marriage.

1448. Write down what you did on all your dates together for an entire year. Read it on New Year's Eve to bring back some wonderful memories.

1449. Create a full life for yourself so that your romantic relationship is the icing on the cake of your life, and not the cake itself.

1450. Take charge of your love life. Create romantic moments instead of just waiting for them to happen. Set some goals. Make some plans.

1451. Know that the most important elements of romance can't be bought with money. Those important elements are:
+ Time   + Affection
+ Appreciation   + Devotion

1452. Spend a rainy Saturday afternoon together creating a photo album out of all of your photographs of the two of you.

1453. Find an autographed copy of her favorite romance novel to give as a remembrance of a special time.

1454. Plan a fantasy trip on the Orient Express or the QE2.

1455. Change your clothes to change your mood. In other words, if you want to feel romantic, dress in a romantic style of clothing.

1456. Start an appreciation campaign. Create a list of reasons that your love should be thrilled to have you as the love of her life. Make it fun, silly, and very upbeat.

1457. Keep track of how much time you actually spend being romantic for one month. How would you rate yourself on the romance scale?

1458. Give him a bottle of "love medicine"—a tiny jar of red hots.

1459. Have an attitude of gratitude for the special relationship you two have been given.

1460. Send a beautiful bouquet of daffodils and tulips on the first day of spring or for the Easter holiday.

1461. Value your partner's feelings even when they differ from your own. Everyone has a right to his or her opinion.

1462. Have a specific time during the workday when both of you say a silent prayer for your relationship.

1463. Visit one of the most romantic places in the United States:
    - ✦ New Orleans
    - ✦ Lake Tahoe
    - ✦ Hawaii
    - ✦ Hilton Head, SC
    - ✦ San Francisco
    - ✦ New York City
    - ✦ Niagara Falls

1464. Create a home filled with love and laughter. Leave negative feelings on the front doorstep.

1465. When going out for a night on the town with your friends and not your lover, give her a long, passionate kiss good-bye. Let her know that you will still be thinking of her.

1466. Keep him company when he is sick. Hang out and spoil him with kindness.

1467. Find out what it takes for your mate to be fulfilled and happy in your relationship. Ask questions. Observe what things make him or her happy.

1468. To put some magic in your relationship, take your love to see a magician's performance.

1469. Take it one day at a time when you are first starting to be romantic. If you try too much, you will burn out and we sure don't want that to happen!

1470. Watch reruns of old romantic comedies together:
      ✦ *I Love Lucy*
      ✦ *The Dick Van Dyke Show*
      ✦ *Mad about You*

1471. Give a box of white chocolates to symbolize the purity of your love.

1472. Give it all you've got by setting the scene for romance in a big way. Go to the most romantic setting that you can find, at the most romantic time of the year, at the most romantic time of night, and declare your love.

Life has no job nobler than that of love.
    —Author Unknown

1473. Become a romance detective to uncover:
      ✦ Your mate's likes and dislikes
      ✦ Current trends in dating
      ✦ Great romantic nightspots
      ✦ Stores that stock romantic gifts

1474. Be sure to touch base with each other throughout the day. Learn to stay connected even when you aren't together.

1475. Look for ways to make both of you feel connected to each other.

1476. Arrange to have a bouquet delivered to your sweetheart's office every hour on her birthday.

1477. Keep in mind that intimacy can take place only when you are able to understand and accept your partner for who he really is.

1478. If you find that your marriage is lacking passion, consider:
      ✦ Taking a mini-vacation
      ✦ Pretending that you aren't married and are having an affair with one another
      ✦ Working hard at becoming more romantic

1479. Know that self-confidence will make up for any lack of physical beauty. Increase your own self-esteem when you want more romance in your life. Look at all of the good things that you have going for yourself. Practice positive self-talk. Pray.

1480. Kissing is one of the most intimate bonds that two lovers can share, so try to be a great kisser. Why not read one of the newest books on the subject? You might just learn a lot!

1481. Remember that sexual contact shouldn't constitute all of your affectionate gestures.

1482. If you are uncomfortable talking about intimate subjects, please note that it gets easier the more you do it.

1483. For women only: Men appreciate intimacy and relationship more as they age. Just imagine what he will be like in ten years!

1484. Decorate your Christmas tree with paper hearts that have love notes written by hand on them. Fill in with little glass heart ornaments to make your tree really special.

1485. Sing "your song" everywhere you go. Get into a romantic mood.

1486. Make the most of springtime, when the whole world falls in love.

1487. Springtime in Paris—need we say more? This is about as romantic as you can ever be!

1488. Visualize your ideal romantic day before hopping out of bed in the morning.

1489. While you are out of town, give her some of your shirts to sleep in to remind her of you.

1490. Before you go on a trip together, get:
    ✦ Special evening clothes
    ✦ Great lingerie
    ✦ Gifts to take along on the trip for your mate as a surprise
    ✦ A city guidebook

1491. Place a Valentine's Day classified ad that tells just how very much you care.

1492. Place a big cupid on your front door and have red arrows leading your mate to find either you or a gift.

1493. Before the two of you head to a romantic ski resort, buy matching goggles and outfits.

1494. Always say "Bless you" when your mate sneezes.

1495. Stay up with your mate when he has insomnia. Fix him some hot chocolate. Chitchat by the fire.

1496. Arrange things so that both of you can be members of the wedding party when your friends get married. Weddings are so romantic.

1497. Keep a piece of your wedding cake in your freezer forever!

1498. If you can't afford some of the more expensive romantic gifts or gestures, focus on the ones you are comfortable with. Don't wait to get started!

1499. Host a lovely champagne brunch for your lover on the weekend.

Love is not blind—it sees more, not less. But because it sees more, it is willing to see less.
—Rabbi Julius Gordon

1500. Three of the worst romance killers:
  ✦ Resentment ✦ Grudge-holding ✦ Jealousy

1501. Copy the romantic gestures of happy couples. Add your personal touches.

1502. Put love notes in plastic Easter eggs and hide them for your lover to find on Easter morning.

1503. Buy a new set of designer sheets for a touch of sophistication in your bedroom.

1504. Occasions to give a stuffed animal:
  ✦ Any occasion: a teddy bear
  ✦ Easter: an Easter bunny
  ✦ Valentine's Day: a cute stuffed toy or Cupid
  ✦ Christmas: an antique teddy
  ✦ Anniversaries (little ones, that is!)
  ✦ When your love is sick
  ✦ When your mate needs a little bit of cheering up

1505. Instead of watching the ball game, tape it, take her out, and watch the game after she goes to bed.

1506. Talk a little "baby talk" to your lover if you get the vibes to do so.

1507. Secretly check his schedule to plan a great time to kidnap him from the office.

1508. Plan a beautiful beach wedding in Hawaii. Plan a renewal of your vows in Hawaii.

1509. Use a soft, special tone of voice when you speak to your lover about your love.

1510. Give him an ice bucket filled with a bottle of good champagne and two crystal flutes.

1511. Get together on a very foggy night and pretend that you are in London.

1512. Resolve old grievances—NOW! Don't let trouble keep brewing.

1513. Your music library should include these romantic styles of music:
    - ✦ Vocal
    - ✦ Instrumental
    - ✦ Classical
    - ✦ Adult contemporary
    - ✦ Top 40

1514. Send anniversary cards on the date of your wedding each month for the entire year.

1515. Give her a diamond anniversary ring that will let her know that you really would marry her all over again. Dazzle her with it.

1516. If she has a favorite work of art and you are unable to buy the original, give her a good copy of it.

1517. When your sister gets married, be sure that your love gets asked to be a bridesmaid.

1518. Explore your spirituality together—it will deepen your relationship.

1519. Carry in the heavy bags of groceries for her and slip a tiny note in the bottom of a bag for her to find when she unpacks them.

1520. Order for her at restaurants that you have been to but she hasn't. Or make suggestions about what she would like.

1521. For a special breakfast, fix heart-shaped:
    + Eggs
    + Pancakes
    + Fruit cutouts
    + Waffles
    + Toast

1522. Make great music together at home by using a karaoke machine and taping your duet.

1523. Prepare a program that lists all the planned events for your very special night out on the town and give it to your lover the day before the big event to create a bit of added excitement about the date.

1524. Go to your library and get some travel guides that are just for couples and get started planning your getaway.

1525. Keep your relationship on the cutting edge by staying up-to-date on the latest:
    + Trends
    + Restaurant openings
    + Products
    + Love songs
    + Styles
    + Romantic best-sellers
    + Events
    + Romantic movies

1526. Keep in mind that picturesque settings often lead to romantic feelings. Set the scene.

1527. Host a little backyard luau together and dress in Hawaiian-style clothing.

1528. Help your mate obtain:
    + Dreams
    + Unique forms of self-expression
    + Goals
    + Personal happiness
    + Success
    + Religious beliefs
    + Recognition

1529. Get your wife and daughter matching mother/daughter outfits.

I like not only to be loved, but also to be told that I am loved.
—George Eliot

1530. If it is too early in the day to toast each other with champagne, toast each other with sparkling water or juice.

1531. Dangerous romance killers:
    + Arrogance
    + Conceit
    + Selfishness
    + Egotism

1532. You should constantly be on the lookout for keepsakes, tokens of love, and souvenirs to buy for your significant other.

1533. Always show your lover:
   ✦ Goodwill   ✦ Kindness   ✦ Tenderness

1534. Give him a model of his dream car with a little note that says "Someday."

1535. Give her a model of her dream house with a note that says "Someday."

1536. Follow in Eve's footsteps, but with a twist; tempt him with a chocolate apple.

1537. Research her family tree and be sure to place your name beside hers.

1538. Take a horseback ride along a beautiful beach together at sunset.

1539. Dance the most romantic of dances, the tango. If you don't know how, take a few lessons. You'll have lots of fun and you will learn to be romantic dancers.

1540. Ask a street musician to play "your song."

1541. Talk on the telephone for hours when you can't be together.

1542. Learn the latest dance steps together.

1543. Start a joint savings account. Save for your future, your dream house, or a once-in-a-lifetime vacation.

1544. Carry an umbrella that is made for two on stormy date nights.

1545. Share a rich milkshake at an old-time diner.

1546. Arrange for a high school band to play "your song" at a local parade. Most band directors will be happy to help out your romantic schemes if you make a nice donation to their band funds.

1547. Create your own "Mirth Days." Think about what makes the two of you happy and then go out and celebrate it.

1548. Get her a new exercise outfit for her aerobics class in a pretty shade of pink or red or with hearts on it.

1549. If your mate has a high-stress career, take him out to the country for a weekend of R and R (romance and relaxation).

1550. Give a gift of a wakeup service to a mate who can't get out of bed in the mornings.

1551. If she mentions that she would love to have a certain style of dress but can't find it, hire a dressmaker to create it for her.

1552. Rent a huge banquet hall and throw a huge party in his honor for no special occasion.

1553. Stroll through an arts and crafts show to look for unique gifts for your mate.

1554. Have elegant engraved invitations made for her surprise party and save one for her scrapbook.

1555. Get a car alarm for his new car. Have it secretly installed and leave a little note telling him that you just wanted to look after his "new love."

1556. If you want to give her a ruby ring or bracelet but find that it is too expensive, give the other popular red stone that costs much less. Give her a garnet.

1557. Present her with a home safe to store her jewelry in and have a lovely piece of jewelry tucked inside for her to find.

> *The one word above all others that makes marriage successful is "ours."*
> —Robert Quillen

1558. Know that sometimes the best friends that the two of you can have are the friends that you make together. Circulate, network, and socialize together to make some wonderful joint new friends.

1559. Keep in mind that your mate doesn't have to love all your friends. Give each other room to have personal friends within the relationship.

1560. Just because the two of you are a couple, don't exclude singles from your social circle. You two need friends of all lifestyles to keep your relationship vital and alive.

1561. When she is in a bad mood, give her some bright wardrobe accents to brighten her spirits.

1562. Give her a new love seat for her living room. Attach a romantic note to it.

1563. Take her to the important fashion shows in:
     ✦ New York   ✦ London   ✦ Paris   ✦ Milan

     Be sure to buy her a new frock or two!

1564. Treat your mate to some status symbols for a touch of glamour.

1565. Slip a sterling silver compact into her cosmetic bag.

1566. Send chocolate truffles instead of a traditional box of chocolates.

1567. Buy a gorgeous crystal chandelier to hang in your bedroom. Be sure to add a dimmer switch to it to set the mood.

1568. Keep a brainstorming list of ways to please your mate. Add to it often and then do the items from it on a regular basis.

1569. Get her favorite celebrity to propose for you or write a love note for you.

1570. If you have messed up, send a "forgive me" bouquet after you make up in person.

1571. Give her a gold key to symbolize that she has the key to your heart.

1572. Rent a cottage in a scenic location for your next vacation. It will be a great way to have some wonderful privacy and a romantic setting.

1573. Reasons to send flowers:
     ✦ It's your first-date anniversary.
     ✦ Your lover is sick.
     ✦ Your lover got a promotion.
     ✦ Your lover has a new home.
     ✦ It's your wedding anniversary.
     ✦ It's your engagement anniversary.
     ✦ It's the first night of your honeymoon.
     ✦ It's the last night of your honeymoon.
     ✦ You've had an argument.
     ✦ Her dog is sick.
     ✦ Her best friend got married and she is single.
     ✦ She had a major fight with a friend or her mom.

1574. Keep in mind that the best reason to send flowers is for no special occasion at all!

1575. Even if you have been married for twenty years, be sure to continue to date each other.

1576. Feed your lover:
- ✦ Chocolates
- ✦ Tropical fruits
- ✦ Gourmet finger foods
- ✦ Your homemade goodies

1577. For men only: Always go to the theater to see the latest romantic movies. Suffer through a chick-flick to be a great romantic.

1578. Rent a great romantic movie for a quiet night at home. Pop some popcorn and snuggle up together.

1579. Imagine that you will never see your lover again and then write a long love letter to her telling her what she has meant to you.

1580. Know the rules for choosing a great restaurant for a romantic evening. Look for one that:
- ✦ Requires dressing up for dinner
- ✦ Is elegant
- ✦ Has candles and flowers on the tables
- ✦ Has fabulous food (especially desserts)
- ✦ Has a fireplace
- ✦ Has dancing

ROMANTIC RULE #9
True romantics understand that time apart from their partners can strengthen and refresh even the best of relationships.

1581. Know that extravagance goes a long, long way in the world of romance. Do not be a penny-pincher!

1582. Learn to speak the language of love—French. Take some classes at a local university or buy a foreign language course to learn at your own pace.

1583. Keep in mind that chivalry is back in style.

1584. Dine by candlelight at least once a week. Even a frozen dinner will taste and look better!

1585. Don't just say you love your mate. Show him in zillions of ways that you love him.

1586. Rules for a night of great romance:
   - ✦ No children
   - ✦ No interruptions
   - ✦ No telephones
   - ✦ No pets
   - ✦ No workplace chitchat

1587. Sometimes one of the best ways to be romantic is to do a simple gesture in a big way. For example, if he likes cigars, send him a year's supply of them.

1588. Look for romantic inspiration everywhere you go. Keep your eyes open and your imagination turned on full-blast.

1589. To make your love feel important, give her your full attention.

1590. Always strive to be the most romantic person in the world! The dividends are priceless.

1591. Plan a weeklong birthday celebration. Bake cupcakes and give him one every day until his birthday, and on his birthday bake a fabulous, heart-shaped birthday cake for him. Place a birthday greeting with each cupcake along with a tiny gift to make the whole week special for him.

1592. If you want to choose a low-cost romantic restaurant, look for:
   - ✦ Quaint neighborhood establishments
   - ✦ Ethnic foods
   - ✦ Dark decor
   - ✦ Good reviews of the cuisine
   - ✦ Recommendations from family and friends who are romantic, but budget conscious

1593. Never allow yourselves to get into a predictable rut where you just keep on doing the same old stuff. Stir things up!

This is the miracle that happens every time to those who really love, the more they give, the more they possess.
—Rainer Maria Rilke

1594. Find a way to share each other's interests and hobbies. Sometimes, a little interest can move a relationship a long, long way.

1595. Call your lover at the office to say:
- ✦ Hurry home.
- ✦ I love you.
- ✦ I miss you.
- ✦ Thanks for last night.
- ✦ Meet me.
- ✦ Let's do something romantic tonight.

1596. Ask a radio disk jockey to dedicate a song to your love. Be sure he or she is listening.

1597. Enter yourselves in a Valentine contest. Radio and television stations are famous for these promotions during the month of February.

1598. Pack a gourmet picnic lunch and take it to her office for a midday touch of romance.

1599. Sing "your song" to her as she falls asleep in your arms tonight.

1600. Pray together for your relationship.

1601. Whisper. Whisper. Whisper. Everything sounds sexier when whispered in a lover's ear.

1602. Spend a lazy summer afternoon in bed. Spend a cold winter morning snuggled up in bed.

1603. Whisk him away on a surprise weekend getaway. You'll need:
- ✦ Hotel accommodations
- ✦ His schedule cleared
- ✦ His suitcase packed
- ✦ Money and credit cards
- ✦ A sense of adventure

1604. The next time you are going away on an extended business trip, give your lover a teddy bear or puppy for company.

1605. Prepare your partner's favorite meal for him. Call his mother to get the recipe if you don't have it.

Love is like quicksilver in the hand.
Leave the fingers open and it stays in the palm;
clutch it and it darts away.
—Dorothy Parker

1606. Qualities for men to cultivate:
- ✦ Chivalry
- ✦ Gallantry
- ✦ Good manners

1607. E-mail him an unexpected love note. Add an element of surprise or mystery to it.

1608. Fax a love letter to your mate. Make it one that he will never forget.

1609. Know your lover's sizes so that you can give the perfect-fitting gift. Carry them in your wallet so that you will have them whenever you shop.

1610. Keep a collection of tapes of romantic music in your car. Play them whenever your mate is with you.

DALE'S PICK FOR BEST/CLASSIC LOVE SONGS:

"In Your Eyes" – Peter Gabriel

"The Power of Love" – Celine Dion

"Don't Know Why" – Norah Jones

"Kiss From a Rose" – Seal

"Here and Now" – Luther Vandross

"From This Moment On" – Shania Twain

"You Make Me Feel Brand New" – Simply Red

"Wind Beneath My Wings" – Bette Midler

"Look Through My Eyes" – Phil Collins

"Reach Out, I'll Be There" – Michael McDonald

1611. Take off your eyeglasses and sunglasses when you kiss.

1612. When you send a greeting card, do it with a little panache:
- ✦ Send more than one.
- ✦ Send a huge card.
- ✦ Send it by registered mail.
- ✦ Send it by a special messenger.
- ✦ Deliver it in person.
- ✦ Stuff her mailbox full of cards.
- ✦ Slide a ton of cards under his door.

1613. Bake a huge chocolate-chip cookie and put a loving message on it with icing.

1614. Make a heart-shaped pizza and spell out "Luv Ya" in pepperoni.

1615. Give a classic romantic CD for a little anniversary gift. Dance to it all night long.

1616. Get out of your dating rut. Choose something that the two of you have never done together from *2002 Things to Do on a Date*. Make plans to do it this coming weekend.

1617. Go out for a fabulous Sunday brunch after church. Make plans for the week ahead while you wait for your food to be served.

1618. Give homemade gifts that speak from the heart. Let your mate see that you care enough to spend lots of time on your gifts.

1619. Meet her for lunch at the mall when she is out on a major day of shopping.

1620. Give her a gift certificate to her favorite store. Wrap it up in a heart-shaped box.

1621. Secretly slip a hundred-dollar bill in her wallet before she goes shopping.

1622. When you set a romantic table, use:
- ✦ The good china
- ✦ Sterling flatware
- ✦ Cloth napkins
- ✦ Candles
- ✦ Tablecloth/placemats
- ✦ A floral centerpiece

1623. Our picks for romantic foods and beverages:
- ✦ Strawberries
- ✦ Chocolates
- ✦ Champagne
- ✦ Wine
- ✦ Caviar
- ✦ Brandy
- ✦ Lobster
- ✦ Grapes

1624. Invest in romance:
- ✦ Diamonds
- ✦ Gold
- ✦ Platinum

1625. Shop for new romantic looks for your home together.

1626. Kiss goodnight. Kiss goodnight every night.

1627. Compliment your mate in public. It doubles the benefits of the compliment.

1628. Purchase a second home for your romantic getaway.

1629. Send a formal invitation through the mail for your next date. Create some ambiance.

1630. Send chocolate roses instead of long-stemmed red ones.

1631. Give a prepaid telephone calling card to your mate the next time she leaves town so that she can call you free of charge.

1632. On your anniversary, go to a craft store and purchase a wedding cake topper and place it proudly on your dessert for a little touch of romance.

1633. Purchase a large coffee-table-sized journal and leave it out for the two of you to jot down your feelings and thoughts about each other whenever the mood strikes. It will be a treasure in the years to come.

1634. Cut out cute romantic cartoons from the newspapers and send them to your mate.

1635. Ask your lover to give you a list of his ten top dream vacation spots. Call your travel agent and turn his dream into a reality.

1636. Have your mate give you a list of her dream gifts. Ask her to update it on a regular basis so that you will always have great ideas for presents.

1637. Send him to a baseball training camp for a week. Halfway through the trip, surprise him by meeting him there and turning the sports trip into a second honeymoon.

1638. Keep a little romantic gift tucked away just in case your romantic mate gives you a gift and you want to reciprocate.

1639. When shopping for anniversary gifts, think:
+ Extra-special
+ Romantic
+ Unique to your partner's tastes
+ Nonpractical
+ Tasteful
+ Meaningful

1640. At the beginning of each month, make a list of romantic gestures and dates that you can do and vow to do them.

1641. Take her on the most popular date in the entire world—go out for dinner.

1642. If you want her to feel sexy, give her a gift certificate to Victoria's Secret.

1643. How to buy elegant gifts on a budget:
+ Shop sales.
+ Shop in advance of the holiday rush.
+ Always be on the lookout for great gifts.
+ Shop outlets.
+ Shop warehouse stores.
+ Shop antiques stores.
+ Browse flea markets.
+ Shop online.
+ Shop at auctions.

1644. Always keep a bottle of champagne on ice just for the little occasions that pop up and need to be celebrated in a special way.

1645. Want to give your love fabulous jewels, but your budget won't allow it? Try a little creative substitution:
+ Instead of cultured pearls, give seed pearls.
+ Instead of a diamond engagement ring, give a birthstone engagement ring.
+ Instead of a gold bracelet, give a sterling silver one.
+ Instead of platinum, give white gold.

1646. If she wants an engagement ring but you aren't ready to make that commitment yet, tell her before the next big holiday that a ring isn't coming as her gift, to save both of you from heartache.

1647. Remember that how you present a gift is almost as important as the gift itself.

1648. Send postcards to your love while you are away on a business trip. Write a little romantic sentiment on it.

1649. Have cute nicknames for each other. Don't use any sarcastic ones.

1650. Visit a honeymoon resort on your next vacation. Ask your travel agent for some great suggestions.

1651. Spend at least one night a year in the bridal suite of a lovely hotel.

1652. Take your lover along on your next business trip. Go out and celebrate in the evenings.

1653. Give her a set of love coupons, which are available at most bookstores and gift shops in early February. Buy a couple of sets and give them throughout the year. Or make your own love coupons.

1654. Call in advance for dates. Yes, you should ask even your marriage partner of fifty years for dates in advance!

1655. Put a great deal of effort into planning your vacations. Turn them into second honeymoons.

1656. Get a part-time job to earn extra money so that you can buy your lover a dream gift.

1657. Write a greeting on your love's morning newspaper. Decorate the paper with hearts.

1658. Look for romantic tips in popular:
- ✦ Magazines
- ✦ Movies
- ✦ Newspapers
- ✦ Television shows
- ✦ Online
- ✦ Books

> *A great lover is one who never loses his childlike heart.*
> —**Author Unknown**

1659. Give her the gift of her favorite fragrance in all its forms:
- ✦ Bath powder
- ✦ Candles
- ✦ Bath gels and oils
- ✦ Lotions

1660. Massage his neck after a stressful day at the office. Make him melt in your arms.

1661. Replace all of the game pieces of her favorite childhood board game with heart-shaped pieces in a variety of colors.

1662. Renew your wedding vows over and over.

1663. Simply read over your wedding vows to refresh your memory about what you promised.

1664. Have Saturday night's dinner catered in your home and enjoy staying in together.

1665. Hire a band or pianist to play for you and your lover at your home.

1666. Fill her glove compartment with flowers. Leave one flower peeking out of the top.

1667. Let him know just how much you appreciate him. Men need to feel appreciated just as much as women do.

1668. Bake your lover a birthday cake. Decorate it with a wonderful theme. Place candles on it and have him make a romantic wish that only you can grant.

1669. If 1668 doesn't work for you, buy your mate a gorgeous birthday cake from the best bakery in town.

1670. Go on a camping trip and enjoy evenings under the stars together.

1671. Send your children to the babysitter's, grandmother's, or a friend's for the weekend.

1672. Create a sense of mystery and excitement when planning your next party. Hire a party planner to get things moving in the right direction.

1673. Prepare an elaborate scavenger hunt for his next birthday. Invite his closest friends and turn it into a memorable event.

1674. Buy your lover a piece of antique jewelry that has a history or romance.

1675. Hide a gift of jewelry in:
     + An ice cube   + A birthday cake

1676. Tuck a small fun gift into a box of Cracker Jack.

1677. Fill the medicine cabinet with heart confetti to start your lover's day off in a romantic way.

1678. Make up a crossword puzzle that highlights your history together.

1679. Create a collage of your relationship. Include all of your special couple events.

1680. To have an interesting beginning to a big date, leave a set of clues to where the date will be and then meet your love there.

1681. Pick wildflowers for her while you are on a picnic.

1682. Give him tickets to a:
+ Sporting event
+ Rock concert
+ Jazz club
+ Fitness club

1683. Give her tickets to the:
+ Opera
+ Symphony
+ Ballet

1684. Make your lover a major priority in your busy life. Let him know how very important he is to you by making lots of time for him.

1685. Send your children over to a friend's house for the afternoon so that you and your spouse can have a little time for romance.

1686. Plant a surprise flower garden for her.

1687. Send flowers to your mate's mother on your mate's birthday. They will both love you for it!

1688. Give her a charm bracelet that consists of charms that hold special meaning for the two of you.

1689. Send your love flowers while you are out of town. Let her know that out of sight doesn't mean out of mind.

1690. Keep a picture of your mate on your desk at the office.

1691. Give her a sterling silver bud vase and promise always to keep a fresh rose in it.

1692. After the next big snowstorm, clean off his windshield in the shape of a heart.

1693. For women only: Seek gift-giving advice from:
+ His dad
+ His mom
+ His coworkers
+ His friends
+ His siblings
+ His boss

1694. For men only: Seek gift-giving advice from:
    ◆ Her best friend   ◆ Her sisters
    ◆ Her mom   ◆ A professional shopper
    ◆ Her coworkers

1695. Get to know your local florist and ask his help in picking out unique floral arrangements.

> *A man should keep his friendships*
> *in constant repair.*
> —Samuel Johnson

1696. While away from your mate, send a bouquet of forget-me-nots.

1697. Buy a "You are special today" plate and use it for your mate's birthdays and your anniversaries.

1698. Visit your local nursery and buy a rose bush that carries her name. Plant it in a place of honor in your yard.

1699. Send your love a box of divinity with a note saying that you think she is heavenly.

1700. Learn to play "your song" on a musical instrument.

1701. Gently wake him with kisses when he snores and keeps you awake.

1702. Send her gourmet lunches every Friday for a year. It is guaranteed to start the weekend off on the right foot.

1703. Pretend that you and your mate won't see each other after tonight. See what happens!

1704. Wrap each of his birthday presents in a different birthday paper to make the gifts look even more special.

1705. Pretend to be:
    ◆ Scarlet and Rhett
    ◆ Tarzan and Jane
    ◆ Romeo and Juliet

> *Love one another. It's as simple*
> *and difficult as that.*
> —Michael Leunig

1706. On momentous birthdays, find greeting cards that acknowledge the years. Send a ton of them to your mate to celebrate the big day.

1707. Pretend to be chained together at the ankles for a Saturday afternoon.

1708. It is very hard to beat a gift of homemade fudge, cookies, or brownies when you want to treat your love. Start your ovens!

1709. Prepare a fabulous Easter basket for your mate. Be sure to include all her childhood favorites and a big stuffed bunny.

1710. Read *In Style* magazine to get ideas on fashionable and trendy ways to show you care.

1711. Every time you pass a candy store, treat your mate to a small box of candy.

1712. Give him a new tie to wear for his next big meeting at work.

1713. Hire an artist to paint a romantic mural on your bedroom wall. What about a beautiful scene from your honeymoon?

1714. Leave her a gift in the baby's room for her to find late at night.

1715. Hire a limousine to bring her home from the office on your anniversary or her birthday.

1716. Keep a diary of your favorite moments together from your lover's birthday to her next birthday. Give it to her for her birthday.

1717. Sign a romantic card "Your secret love" just to spice things up a bit.

1718. Break out the fabulous bottle of wine that you have been saving for a special occasion and turn tonight into a special evening for two.

1719. Take a no-cost vacation for two. Stay at a friend's vacation home or visit your parents.

1720. Show up on his commuter ride home from the office with a romantic letter and candy.

1721. When planning a getaway, check out the low weekend rates offered at most major hotel chains. Ask for special honeymoon offers, too.

1722. Read the reviews of new restaurants, plays, and shows to look for exciting date ideas.

1723. Smile warmly at your lover. Show her how you feel.

1724. Start a romance fund. Save for a fabulous honeymoon, second honeymoon, or vacation getaway.

1725. Buy an RV and turn it into your love nest on wheels. Set out and see the world together.

1726. Start little holiday traditions:
  + Preparing holiday meals together
  + Fixing a Christmas stocking for each other
  + Trimming a tree together
  + Carving a pumpkin for Halloween together
  + Decorating Easter eggs together
  + Having your own fireworks on July 4th
  + Going on lots of summer picnics
  + Throwing birthday parties for friends and family
  + Hosting a big backyard barbecue

ROMANTIC RULE #10
Romance isn't dependent on age, marital status, or gender.
Anyone who wants to be romantic can be if he or she works at it.

1727. Walk down the street arm-in-arm and show the world that you are a couple.

1728. Spend the night at a romantic ski resort. Be sure to reserve a room with a great view.

1729. Learn to communicate well with your mate. Read the current bestsellers on relationship issues to gain some great insights on quality communication.

1730. Take a massage class. Learn this art of relaxation. Consider taking the class together.

1731. Use a love poem as a bookmark.

1732. Stop by the nearest gift shop and purchase lots of wonderfully scented candles to light up your love life.

1733. Tape inspirational relationship messages on your bathroom mirror.

1734. Indulge your chocolate-loving mate by serving a yummy chocolate milk shake or baking a wonderful chocolate cake, chocolate cheesecake, chocolate cream pie, or chocolate-chip cookies.

1735. "Toe snuggle" under the covers.

1736. Treat her to breakfast, lunch, and dinner in bed whenever she is sick.

1737. Add a touch of glamour to her flannel nightgown. Hang a feather boa next to it.

1738. Tell your love to reserve a specific date at a specific time, but don't say why. Then surprise him with tickets to a fabulous sold-out show.

1739. Spoil him by doing all his least favorite chores for him.

1740. On birthday and anniversary cakes, use sparklers instead of candles.

1741. Give her some gifts to make her feel glamorous:
- ✦ Gift certificate to a spa
- ✦ Beauty treatments
- ✦ Designer clothes
- ✦ Gorgeous silk lingerie
- ✦ Beautiful gold or diamond jewelry

1742. Instead of sending a birthday card, send a:
- ✦ Birthday poem
- ✦ Singing telegram
- ✦ Cake delivered by messenger
- ✦ Musical card
- ✦ Balloon bouquet

1743. Be sure that you celebrate both your engagement and wedding anniversaries.

1744. Stop by the liquor store and pick up a bottle of fine brandy to sip in front of the fire.

1745. On your mate's birthday, give a scrapbook of all your shared birthday celebrations. It will bring back some wonderful memories.

1746. On your anniversary, send her one bouquet for each year that you have been married.

1747. Want to make Mr. Hallmark happy? Send one romantic greeting card for each date that the two of you have shared. Make all of them romantic ones.

1748. Bring home his favorite beverage and appetizer for a nice happy hour for two.

1749. Stop by the best deli and pick up her favorite dessert for dinner tonight.

1750. Celebrate the first day of each new season by sending a seasonal bouquet and greeting card.

The remembrance of the good done to those we have loved is the only consolation left us when we have lost them.
—Demoustier

1751. If you can't write poetry, borrow from the masters, such as Browning and Shakespeare.

1752. Always make an extra effort to be caring when your mate is sick:
- ✦ Send flowers.
- ✦ Send a get well card.
- ✦ Prepare homemade soup.
- ✦ Bring magazines and books.
- ✦ Take him to the doctor.
- ✦ Rent some DVDs for him.

1753. Take a walk with your sweetheart in the first snowfall of the season. Create a heart snow sculpture or two snow people who look like a couple of lovebirds.

1754. Make plans together for every major holiday. Create some wonderful memories.

1755. Create your own personalized greeting card. These are available at most large card shops.

1756. Plan a romantic trip to a well-known honeymoon area for a weekend getaway:
- ✦ The Poconos
- ✦ Niagara Falls
- ✦ Great Smoky Mountains

1757. Send your love a romantic novel and make the most romantic part of the book your wildly romantic inscription.

1758. On a cold night, stay at home and snuggle under the covers.

1759. Unplug the television. See what happens! Try it for a night, week, month, or year! How long can the two of you go without watching television?

1760. Give him a hand massage after he has been working hard with his hands.

1761. On an extremely cold morning, warm up her car for her before she leaves for the office.

1762. While your mate is in the shower, warm his towel in the dryer and hide a little love note inside the folded towel. Or treat him to a towel warmer for the bathroom.

1763. Put confetti in greeting cards and also enclose some new pictures of the two of you.

1764. Create new lines to the old poem:

Roses are red,
Violets are blue,
Sugar is sweet
And so are you.

Create a new line to any love poem. You don't even need to be a poet. Anyone can write a new line or two.

1765. Laugh together OFTEN. A sense of humor can be very romantic.

1766. Send silly romantic jokes to each other just to brighten the day.

1767. Have your own couple's list of your favorite:
- Restaurants
- Beverages
- Shows
- Songs
- Vacation spots
- Recording artists
- Activities
- Artists
- Movies

1768. Give her a subscription to a bridal magazine just because she was once your bride. Give her one when your daughter is planning her wedding.

1769. If you aren't ready to give her a diamond ring, how about giving a diamond of another style? We suggest:
- Earrings
- Tennis bracelet
- Pendant
- Right-hand ring

1770. Surprise her by having dinner ready for her when she gets home tonight.

1771. Purchase all new ornaments for her Christmas tree. Select a romantic theme for the decorations.

1772. Recycle your love:
- Reread your old love letters from each other.
- Re-create your first date.
- Re-create your best date.
- Reread your favorite love story.

The more you are motivated by love, the more fearless and free your actions will be.
—Dalai Lama

1773. To make a lovely picture of romance, frame:
- Your favorite romantic CD cover
- A love poem
- A love letter
- A photo of the two of you
- Your baby bracelets together
- Menus from romantic dinners you have shared
- Your wedding license
- Romantic cartoons
- Travel posters from your honeymoon
- Programs from romantic plays and musicals

At the touch of love, everyone becomes a poet.
—Plato

1774. Fall into a pile of fall leaves together. Frolic. Play together.

1775. On New Year's Eve and your anniversary eve, make relationship resolutions together.

1776. Fix a memorabilia box of your relationship. Include:

Photos	Hotel room keys	Poems
Ticket stubs	Dried flowers	
Cards	Love letters	

1777. Hire a talented local artist to paint a romantic motto on your fireplace mantel. Our favorite: "Fairy tales do come true."

1778. Give her a small gift bag filled with seven kinds of bubble bath, one for every night of the week.

1779. Take him out to dinner at a wonderfully romantic French restaurant. Reserve the most romantic table in the entire restaurant.

1780. Restaurant-hop for a little change. Pick the three most romantic restaurants that you know and have appetizers at one, dinner at another, and dessert at another.

1781. If you want a fabulous romantic setting to propose, take your love to one of the largest and loveliest mansions in the country that is open to the public: Vizcaya, in Miami.

1782. Write a journal of the funny things that happen in your relationship and give it to your mate when he needs a little cheering up.

1783. Forget old arguments and hurts in addition to forgiving your mate.

1784. Get rid of all unromantic relationship habits, such as:
    ✦ Yelling   ✦ Complaining   ✦ Nit-picking
    ✦ Nagging   ✦ Whining   ✦ Fault-finding
    ✦ Name-calling

1785. Discuss what a quality relationship means to both of you. Listen and learn.

1786. If you have a routine dinner planned for tonight, spruce it up by changing the atmosphere to one of romance. Use:
    ✦ Soft lighting   ✦ Candles
    ✦ Mood music   ✦ Loving words

1787. Talk about your values, beliefs, ideas, and philosophies with each other.

1788. Plan big dates far, far in advance to give you both something to look forward to.

1789. Buy a lottery ticket together and agree to spend your winnings in only romantic ways.

1790. Shop together for clothing styles that are pleasing to both of you. Shop for styles that look good together when the two of you are out on the town.

1791. Keep in mind that people on their deathbeds never wish that they had spent more time at the office, but many wish that they had spent more time with their loved ones.

1792. Take a class together one night a week in:
   - ✦ Wine tasting
   - ✦ A foreign language
   - ✦ Gourmet cooking
   - ✦ Ice-skating
   - ✦ Dog obedience
   - ✦ Bible study
   - ✦ Creative writing
   - ✦ Parenting

   It will do your relationship a lot of good to have a shared activity that takes place on a regular basis, outside of your normal date night. It will give you a shared new interest, plus new things to talk about on your dates.

1793. Key phrases in romantic relationships:
   - ✦ "I am very sorry."
   - ✦ "Forgive me."
   - ✦ "I love you."
   - ✦ "I need you."
   - ✦ "Thank you."
   - ✦ "I want you."
   - ✦ "Please."

1794. Kiss whenever you hear your secret code word. Yes, you need first to choose a romantic code word.

1795. Know that your lover is not a mind reader. Speak up and make your thoughts known.

1796. Make a toast to your lover at dinner tonight. Make it memorable.

1797. Strike up your own conversation in an Internet chat room that your mate frequents.

1798. Listen to your mate with your ears and your heart open.

1799. Learn to read your mate's body language. Get a book on the subject the next time you are at a bookstore.

1800. Frame his childhood baseball mitt in a shadow box for his office.

ROMANTIC RULE #11
True romance is putting the happiness of your
significant other ahead of your own happiness.

1801. Attach a note to her car clock asking her to meet you at a specific time for a fabulous date.

1802. Trade romantic ideas with a trusted coworker. Who knows what you might learn!

*Keep your eyes wide open before marriage,
and half-shut afterwards.*
—Benjamin Franklin

1803. Whenever you dine at a restaurant that has a little gift shop, pick up a little trinket such as a box of candy for your mate.

1804. Turn your grandmother's engagement ring into a drop pendant for her.

1805. Give her the most beautiful engagement ring you can afford. This is a ring that she will wear for the rest of her life, so spoil her a bit.

1806. Try to perform a new romantic gesture each week for a year. Are you feeling really romantic? Try a new gesture twice weekly.

1807. Sing "your song" in the shower, as you get ready for a big night out.

1808. Give him a pair of stylish silk boxers for every day of the week or for every holiday.

1809. When he is out with the guys, arrange to have his favorite cocktail brought to him with your sentiments written on a napkin.

1810. Learn to use sign language so that you can send each other loving messages in a new way.

1811. Send your love a love letter from Santa Claus, Indiana, during the holidays. Contact the post office there for details.

1812. Give her a fabulous gift when she has a baby. When you give it to her, turn it into an event. Treat her like a queen.

1813. If you have small children, always get her a Mother's Day gift from the children.

1814. If you have small children, always get him a Father's Day gift from the children.

1815. Decorate his office in a personal style by framing his:
   + Diplomas and certificates   + Boy Scout badges
   + Medals   + Baseball cards

1816. Play the game of Twister together. Act silly. Be childlike.

1817. Make a daily calendar for her by buying a plain one and writing romantic thoughts for each day of the year. Present her with it on New Year's Day.

1818. When you can't kiss because one of you is sick, give each other chocolate kisses.

1819. If your mate isn't the romantic type, set an example through all your romantic gestures.

1820. Tell your mate that you want him to be romantic. Share with him that it is important to you.

1821. Consider getting professional counseling to tweak your relationship.

1822. Always take advantage of a great dance band.

1823. Have a heart-to-heart talk with your lover.

1824. Buy his-and-her towels for your master bathroom.

1825. Entertain the kids when she is sick. Let her get some well-deserved rest and relaxation.

> *In every living thing there is the desire for love.*
> —D.H. Lawrence

1826. Give your mate your wedding invitation framed in a lovely sterling silver frame.

1827. Frame your favorite playbills to hang on the wall in your den.

1828. Frame concert tickets that hold special memories for the two of you.

1829. Give her a lovely bride doll for an anniversary gift if she loved dolls as a child.

1830. Buy some stock in a diamond mine for him.

1831. Ingredients of a romantic dinner:
    - ✦ Cocktail
    - ✦ Gourmet food
    - ✦ Appetizer
    - ✦ Yummy dessert
    - ✦ Fine wine
    - ✦ After-dinner liqueur

1832. Turn your anniversary into a weeklong celebration.

1833. Plan to take your love to a romantic community theater production.

1834. Take a trip to Quebec City, Canada, for the wintertime festivities.

1835. Make a slide-show presentation of your relationship for your significant other.

1836. Send her a lifetime subscription to her favorite magazine.

1837. Read the travel ads in bridal magazines to get ideas for a romantic getaway.

1838. Treat yourself to some fabulous French lingerie.

1839. Slowly kiss the nape of your lover's neck.

1840. Leave a romantic, fun message at the hotel desk when he is out of town on a business trip.

1841. Listen to traditional wedding music as you fall asleep on your anniversary.

1842. Make a cassette tape of all your favorite love songs.

1843. Wash your car before a big date. Take pride in how your car looks for your evening out on the town.

1844. Hang a Welcome Home banner when he comes home from a trip. Show him that you really missed him in a big way.

1845. Each Christmas, go out and buy a special romantic ornament together.

The only gift is a portion of thyself.
—Ralph Waldo Emerson

1846. Share a sleeping bag under the stars in your own backyard.

1847. Renew your vows in a flashy Las Vegas wedding chapel. Call ahead to reserve the chapel of your choice.

1848. Stroll along a deserted beach in the wintertime with your mate. Share stories and dreams.

1849. Serve fruit, fine cheese, and champagne in bed tonight.

1850. After a bad day, cry on his shoulder. Comfort her when she cries.

1851. Browse through the travel section of a large city's newspaper and plan a quick trip together.

1852. Hold hands during dinner. Play footsies during dessert. Liven things up a bit.

1853. Dine at quaint outdoor cafés when the weather permits.

1854. Choose spending time with her over spending time with the guys, and let her know of your choice.

1855. Give your mate your undivided attention. Learn to be a great listener.

1856. Stay up together to watch the last burning ember die out in the fire.

1857. Give him a jukebox filled with the songs that have special meaning for the two of you.

1858. Find a lovely pillow that has a romantic saying on it. Surprise her with it.

1859. Have a special bouquet of flowers waiting for her at your table when you arrive at the restaurant.

1860. Pretend that:
- Your television doesn't work.
- Your phone cable has been cut.
- Your lights work only on the dimmer switch.
- You can't go outside because of bad weather.
- You only have tonight together.

Looking back, I have this to regret, that too often when I loved, I did not say so.
—David Grayson

1861. When you dine out, ask for booths, corner tables, dark tables, or tables with a view, to make your evening out more romantic.

1862. On a cold evening, head over to a quaint coffeehouse and spend an hour talking over a steaming cup of java.

1863. The next time she has a big presentation at work, wait in her office to find out how she did on it.

1864. Give your love a copy of her favorite romantic movie. Promise to watch it with her.

1865. Take ballroom dance lessons together. Is there anything more romantic than a couple that can dance well together?

1866. Treat him to a big, comfortable easy chair to watch his ball games in on Saturday afternoons.

1867. Save your marriage—buy a dual-control electric blanket.

1868. Always date your love notes that you hide just in case they aren't found for a very long time.

1869. Give her an old-fashioned Raggedy Ann doll. It is the only doll that has a heart.

1870. Buy matching PJs and robes to lounge around in on the weekends.

1871. Pack him a gourmet lunch for the next time he has to travel by plane to save him from the airline's food.

1872. Read a quality book about improving your sex life.

1873. Make yourself sexier:
    + Lose weight.
    + Exercise.
    + Get a new wardrobe.
    + Purchase some new lingerie.
    + Try a new hairstyle or hair color.
    + Increase your self-esteem.

1874. If you have had some problems in the past, agree to start the relationship over. A fresh start may be exactly what the two of you need to make a success of your relationship.

1875. Float a love note in a bottle in her bath tonight.

1876. Learn to let go of some of your inhibitions.

1877. Look at your love life. Ask yourself if your love life gets enough of your attention.

1878. Make an adventure out of your next vacation. Go on a romantic African safari.

1879. Spend the next twenty-four hours in bed. Order out for food. Why not make things all hot and spicy between the two of you by ordering Indian food?

1880. Frame a favorite romantic movie poster for some inexpensive art.

1881. Buy a calendar for your mate and fill it with all kinds of dates for the two of you to share. You can mark it with just time for the two of you or specific dates, such as:
    + Dinners   + Movies   + Picnics
    + Concerts   + Ball games

1882. Collect great romantic quotes and turn them into a book for your significant other.

1883. Have a silk floral bouquet made to look like her bridal bouquet and have it placed in a lovely mahogany shadow box to give her for an anniversary gift.

1884. Put a great deal of effort into planning all of your dates.

1885. Take the television out of the bedroom. Replace it with a great sound system to play romantic music.

1886. Host a picnic in your bedroom. Fill a basket with champagne, flowers, candy, gourmet foods, and soft music.

1887. Imagine wonderful things happening between the two of you. Practice positive thinking.

1888. Get stuck in a revolving door together. Kiss discreetly.

1889. Give him a tape of his favorite ball game for a thoughtful "little" anniversary gift.

1890. Hold hands during an airplane trip. Keep each other calm in a storm.

1891. Enjoy your shared history together. Isn't it nice to be with someone who knows all about you?

1892. Try to find a popular song that has your lover's name in it. Play it on your next date.

1893. Get a matchbook from his favorite restaurant and wrap it up with a note inviting him to dinner there.

> *There's always room for love. You just have to move a few things around.*
> —**Anonymous**

1894. Meet for a middle-of-the-night meal. Dine by candlelight.

1895. Learn the art of calligraphy so that you can make your love letters look wonderfully romantic.

1896. Frame the wedding vows from the ceremony when you renewed your vows.

1897. Have a poster-size enlargement made of your favorite photo of the two of you. Frame it for an anniversary gift.

1898. Give her scented liners for her lingerie drawers.

1899. Have a fabulous piece of jewelry designed especially for her.

1900. Give him a gold watch for a milestone birthday or anniversary. Have it engraved with a romantic message on the back.

1901. "TP" his front yard and leave a romantic note. His neighbors will enjoy the show.

1902. Kidnap your lover away from the office for:
   ✦ Lunch
   ✦ An afternoon rendezvous
   ✦ A getaway
   ✦ A romantic date

1903. Let your love know your:
   ✦ Fears   ✦ Hopes   ✦ Secrets   ✦ Desires

1904. Fill her shoes with gift certificates for pedicures or foot massages.

1905. Name your puppy for your mate.

1906. Fill her handbag with new bills or a lovely billfold.

1907. Hang a streamer from the front porch declaring your love.

1908. On your lover's birthday, take her out for breakfast, lunch, and dinner.

1909. When she leaves the table at a restaurant to powder her nose, place a small but special gift at her place.

1910. Keep in mind that bridal magazines are a great source of ideas for romantic home decor and gift-giving.

1911. Use pink light bulbs for romantic lighting. It is much more flattering than regular lighting.

1912. True romance = one love, one lifetime. It is that simple!

1913. Check with local inns, B&Bs, and hotels for their specials for nights out on the town.

1914. Run off together to live on a tropical island at least for a week.

1915. Make every day a day to express your love. Make every day a day to impress your love.

1916. Great places to hide a gift so that your mate won't find it until the big celebration:
    ✦ Behind the refrigerator
    ✦ In the freezer in your garage
    ✦ In your tool shed or garage storage area
    ✦ In the guest bedroom closet
    ✦ In the bottom of the clothes hamper
    ✦ In the trunk of your car
    ✦ Behind seldom-read books on a bookshelf
    ✦ Taped to the back of a picture
    ✦ In the sleeve of a seldom-worn coat
    ✦ At your parents' home
    ✦ At your office
    ✦ At a friend's home
    ✦ At a neighbor's home

1917. Plan a scavenger hunt for your mate to find you. Turn it into an elaborate, fun adventure. Be creative. Make it into a celebration when she finds you.

1918. To get fresh ideas on romance, browse at bookstores in areas such as:

- ✦ Home decorating
- ✦ Psychology
- ✦ Relationships
- ✦ Gift sections
- ✦ Magazines
- ✦ Foreign newspapers
- ✦ Foreign magazines

1919. Make up a romantic dartboard and let your love take aim to win a gift or kiss.

1920. Take her to Chinatown or a great Chinese restaurant to celebrate the Chinese New Year.

1921. Set up your own toll-free telephone number for your love to call you if she travels a lot.

1922. Hire a butler for her for a week, a month, or even a lifetime!

1923. Decorate her bicycle or car with hearts. Leave a big banner across the bike's handlebars.

1924. Two characteristics of great partners:

- ✦ Passionate
- ✦ Compassionate

Ask yourself if you possess these qualities.

1925. For country-oriented lovers, give the latest romantic CD collection.

In love, as in politics, it is always a "third party" that stirs up all the trouble—and throws the machinery out of order.
—**Author Unknown**

1926. Reasons to throw her a party:

- ✦ She received a promotion at work.
- ✦ She has a new hairstyle.
- ✦ She's having a bad hair day.
- ✦ Her best friend got married and she is single.
- ✦ She is pregnant.
- ✦ You love her.
- ✦ It is her birthday.
- ✦ You just got engaged.
- ✦ You want all of your friends to meet her.

1927. Reasons to throw him a party:
  - ✦ He received a promotion at work.
  - ✦ You want a bon voyage party before his big trip.
  - ✦ There is a big game on television.
  - ✦ He finished a project.
  - ✦ It is his birthday.
  - ✦ He got a dog.
  - ✦ He is going to be a dad.
  - ✦ He needs some cheering up.

1928. Learn couples' ice-skating or roller-skating. Take lessons together. Practice together.

1929. Try giving unconditional love to your mate. It isn't always easy, but try.

1930. Buy a bride-and-groom toasting set and make a very special toast to your love on your next anniversary.

1931. True romance is made up of:
  - ✦ Feelings
  - ✦ Intimacies exchanged
  - ✦ Gestures
  - ✦ Total commitment

1932. Stop eating out together at typical cookie-cutter chain restaurants. Start looking for romantic spots to dine at together. Break free from the mundane.

1933. When you are away on business, call her every night at bedtime. Be one of the last things that she thinks about before she drifts off to sleep.

1934. Put your arm around her at the movies. Share your popcorn. Flirt with each other before the show starts.

1935. Compliment her hairstyle every single time she comes home from the salon.

1936. Hire a violinist to play during a romantic dinner. Check with the restaurant beforehand to arrange things or have a musician come to your home to play during a special meal.

1937. Surprise her by bringing along her family on your next vacation.

1938. If you are a bad dancer, secretly sign up for dance lessons. Surprise your mate by taking her out for a fabulous night of dancing after you have completed the lessons.

1939. Learn how to quickly reconnect after being apart during the day. Find out what makes your mate's heart melt and then do it.

1940. Avoid letting fear and embarrassment stop you from expressing your feelings and desires.

1941. Flirt with your mate even if you have been together for decades. Slip into something sexy that he has never seen before when he comes home from work. Knock his socks off!

1942. If you need help with your sex life, send a SASE to the Association of Sex Educators, Counselors, Therapists, PO Box 238, Mt. Vernon, IA 52314 for a referral to a qualified therapist in your area.

ROMANTIC RULE #12
True romantics seek professional help when it is needed.

1943. Get on the mailing lists of unique mail-order catalogs so that you can search out special gifts for your lover.

1944. Create four seasons of photographs of the two of you and change them with the arrival of each new season.

1945. Make love before bedtime. Don't wait till you are both tired.

1946. On your anniversary, recite the lyrics to "your song." Look her in the eyes. Say the words with feeling.

1947. Give her a list of the ten reasons that you love her more than any other person in the world.

1948. Write a five-page letter telling your love your recollections of:
- ✦ Your first meeting
- ✦ Your first date
- ✦ Your first kiss
- ✦ The moment you fell in love
- ✦ Your courtship
- ✦ Your engagement
- ✦ Your wedding
- ✦ Your honeymoon

1949. Snuggle before going to sleep each and every night.

*Letters that should never have been
written and ought immediately to be
destroyed are the only ones worth keeping.*
—Sydney Tremayne

1950. Give up trying to change your mate. Instead, try improving yourself. Your mate will appreciate your efforts and your relationship will improve.

1951. Put your feelings on a theater marquee. Be bold and creative.

1952. Consider buying her a diamond in each of the most popular cuts:
   ✦ Round   ✦ Pear   ✦ Emerald   ✦ Marquee

1953. Hire a skywriter to declare your love.

1954. Place your feelings up for the world to see on a rented billboard.

1955. Make a videotape of you declaring your love for your sweetheart. Don't worry if it is corny. Relax and have fun with it.

1956. Know that there is no substitute for togetherness. Always make time for your significant other even if your work schedule is crazy at the moment.

1957. Hide a diamond ring in the center of a rose bud. Use tweezers to insert it.

1958. During the commercials before a movie, place an ad declaring your love. Check with your local cinema to learn which one has commercial time for rent.

1959. Carve your initials on an old tree (be careful not to cut too deep or you will have the environmentalists after us).

1960. Fly a kite that tells her how you feel. Make your own kite or creatively put your feelings on one so that she will see your love floating high in the sky on the next windy day.

1961. Dance to swing music. It'll put you both in a fun, crazy, romantic mood.

1962. Save all the corks from the champagne bottles that you have shared with your love. Add ribbon and beads and string them together for a unique, romantic garland for your Christmas tree.

1963. Develop gift finesse. Buy clothing for your love that is:
+ In the correct size
+ From your love's favorite store
+ The correct color
+ A flattering style for your love
+ The newest trend
+ A little bit nicer than she usually buys

1964. If you mess up and forget a birthday or an anniversary, admit your mistake. Then make arrangements to celebrate the occasion in a manner that will be twice as nice as it would have been.

1965. Take your mate out for breakfast before work for a great romantic way to start the day.

1966. Make a list of five romantic restaurants that you and your lover haven't been to and vow to visit each one within the next few months.

1967. When you take your love out to dinner, have a gift waiting for her at the table. Surprise her with your thoughtfulness.

1968. Get lost together on purpose for a little romantic adventure.

1969. Take a horse-drawn carriage ride at sunset or on a moonlit night.

1970. Search through your newspaper's classified ads for tickets to sold out events.

1971. Never interrupt your phone calls with your lover to take other calls. Make him feel important at all times.

1972. Find out where she is staying on her business trip and have flowers waiting in her room. Be sure to include a romantic note with them.

1973. Ask your secretary, mom, friend, or coworker to remind you of all your important romantic anniversaries.

1974. Give your mate a gift certificate for lessons as an anniversary bonus gift. We suggest:
+ Golf   + Tennis   + Music   + Swimming

These are all activities that you can enjoy together!

> *The greatest healing therapy*
> *is friendship and love.*
> —Hubert Humphrey

1975. Leave a trail of his favorite candy to lead him to a present or to you!

1976. Declare your feelings of love for your mate in a window display at a lovely store. Call the display director at the nicest department store or specialty shop in town and ask for her help. Most people are glad to help others in the love life department.

1977. At the beginning of each year, look through the new phone book for new restaurants that might be great romantic haunts for the two of you.

1978. Send your wife flowers on your children's birthdays. Send bouquets that are made up of flowers of her birth month.

1979. Great inexpensive "anniversary" gifts:

- ✦ Love stories
- ✦ Heart-shaped puzzles
- ✦ Bottles of wine
- ✦ Gourmet cookies
- ✦ Movie tickets
- ✦ CDs
- ✦ Photo albums
- ✦ Trinket boxes
- ✦ Heart-shaped pillows
- ✦ Lace garments
- ✦ Perfume bottles
- ✦ Plants
- ✦ Flowers
- ✦ T-shirts
- ✦ Key chains
- ✦ Ornaments
- ✦ Self-help tapes
- ✦ Candy
- ✦ DVDs

1980. Ask your lover for a current picture to place on your nightstand.

1981. Gaze into each other's eyes. You might see something in them that you have never noticed before. Remember that the eyes are the windows to the soul.

1982. In the middle of a party, a movie, a dinner, or a chore, whisper something romantic to your lover.

1983. Stop by a Crabtree & Evelyn shop to pick up a sweet-smelling little gift for your love.

1984. Turn your bedroom into a romantic escape, not a TV room and exercise-equipment warehouse. Make this room the most romantic one in the house.

1985. Create a time capsule of your relationship. Bury it in your backyard or favorite park. Vow to be together in twenty years when you dig it up.

1986. Return to the basics of an old-fashioned romance.
- Dignity
- Rituals
- Manners
- Monogamy
- Courting
- Vows kept

*The only things in life you regret
are the risks you didn't take.*
—Anonymous

1987. Meditate on I Corinthians 13 and just watch how your relationship improves!

1988. Read lots of books on social customs and entertaining to get new ideas for creating romance.

1989. Keep in mind that the old saying "Little things mean a lot" is especially true when it comes to romance.

1990. Pick out a constellation together and whenever you see it, think of your mate.

1991. Reasons to be romantic:
- It will enhance your love life.
- It will bring you and your mate closer.
- It is fun and exciting.
- You will be the envy of other couples.
- Your sex life will improve.
- You will be happier in your relationship.
- Your chances of a breakup will drastically diminish.
- You will become a more passionate couple.
- You will be a great role model for your children.

1992. The most popular Valentine gifts:
- Flowers
- Candy
- Lingerie
- Perfume

1993. Ask yourself what changes you would make in your relationship if you had only one more year to live. Start making those changes today. Take advantage of the present to make your future together brighter.

1994. On a cold night when he is working late at the office, bring him a thermos of hot chocolate and some heart-shaped chocolate-chip cookies.

1995. Choose a pendant or earrings that match the color of her eyes. For example:
   + Emeralds for green eyes
   + Sapphires for blue eyes
   + Tiger eyes for brown eyes

1996. Have a red anniversary:
   + Red roses
   + Bottle of red wine
   + Ruby ring
   + Red silk nightgown and robe
   + Ruby red slippers
   + Red dress
   + Ruby bracelet
   + Red cashmere sweater
   + Red muffler

True love doesn't have an ending.
   —Author Unknown

1997. Restrain yourself from buying practical gifts unless they are requested. Even then, be sure to give a second little gift that means romance just to keep your relationship on the romance track.

1998. Name your yacht, car, or airplane for your lover.

1999. Send her a beautiful jewelry box filled with costume jewelry or, better yet, the real stuff!

2000. Celebrate February 29 in a way that she will remember for the next four years. Splurge! Plan! Get out of the box! Go romantically wild!

2001. Appreciate all the differences between men and women instead of complaining about them.

2002. Honor, cherish, love, respect, comfort, and keep your mate, and everything will fall into its romantic place.

The man and woman who can laugh
at their love, who can kiss with smiles and
embrace with chuckles, will outlast in
mutual affection all the throat-lumpy,
cow-eyed couples of their acquaintance.
Nothing lives on so fresh and evergreen
as the love with a funnybone.
—George Jean Nathan

RESOURCES

#19 Romantic Homes
Call 800-883-8851

#203 Council on Foundations
Call 202-467-0427

#420 M&Ms
Call 800-627-7852
www.mms.com

#507 Rosemary's Porcelain Art
599 266th Road
Milford, NE 68405

#768 Condor Flag Company
Call 800-342-3524

#804 De Beers
www.debeers.com

#815 Smitten Mittens
www.smittenmittens.com

#841 Pelham Hotel
15 Cromwell Place
South Kensington Place
London, England
Call 800-553-6674
www.firmdale.com/
pelham.html

#877 Country Living Travel
Call 888-268-9584

#1133 Cumberland Falls State Park
Call 606-528-4124

#1146 Victoria
PO Box 7150
Red Oak, Iowa 51591

#1312 Cash's of Ireland
Call 800-223-8100

ABOUT THE AUTHORS

Cyndi Haynes and Dale Edwards wrote their first book, *2002 Things to Do on a Date,* when they were dating. They continued to write together and married just before their second book was published. The couple has appeared on hundreds of radio and television programs. Their books have been written about in numerous publications including *Redbook, Cosmopolitan,* and *Marie Claire.* Their books have been published in a dozen foreign languages. They live in Indiana with their son and three big dogs.

Books by Cyndi Haynes

1000 Best Dating Secrets
Luv Questions
Keeping Love Alive
The Book of Friendship

The Book of Change
2002 Ways to Cheer Yourself Up
2002 Ways to Show Your Kids You Love
  Them

Other Books by Cyndi Haynes and Dale Edwards

2002 Ways to Find, Attract,
  and Keep a Mate

2002 Things to Do on a Date